LETTERS FROM ICELAND 1936

By

Jean Young

The University of Birmingham
School of English
1992

© Marion Agnes Harvey 1992

ISBN: 0 7044 1247 0

Printed in the University of Birmingham

FOREWORD

Jean Young became interested in Scandinavian languages and literature while studying for the English tripos at Girton College, Cambridge, beginning in the autumn of 1921. Her post-graduate work in Dublin was concerned with literary relations between Icelandic and Irish literature. A few years later she became a lecturer in English at Reading University where she worked until her retirement.

She made a number of translations, on her own or in collaboration with others, from Scandinavian languages and some of her research was concerned with Old Icelandic literature. In 1936 she realised her long-held desire to visit Iceland. These letters were written to her family while she was on that visit, and form a fascinating record of her first impressions and developing understanding of a country the literature of which remained to the end of her life one of her greatest interests, as well as acounts of the many people she met there, such as the Icelandic-Swedish Astrid, related to the Blöndals, whom she had got to know, together with her sister Hildur, when working in Sweden in the 1920s.

The letters were transcribed by Eleanor Haworth, one of Jean's life-long friends, typed into a word-processor by Ian Wyatt, formerly a student of Old Icelandic at Birmingham University, and edited by Anthony Faulkes. They have been reproduced in a form as close as possible to the originals, and the quirks of spelling and punctuation of the originals have been retained; nor has any attempt been made to correct the spellings of Icelandic words and names or the identifications of birds, plants and rocks. Abbreviations have also been left as they are, and are mostly self-explanatory (mg = morning, mts = mountains, sg = something, sts = sometimes, cy = company, jy = journey, ∵ = because, c. = circa (i.e. about), etc.). A few short passages of purely personal matters have been omitted and are marked by . . . The occasional sketches have been reproduced electronically, as have a few of the prints of snapshots that Jean took on her travels; the photographs reproduced as plates between pp. 36 and 37 and on p. 76 are reproduced from a set of glass slides that she had made.

I

> Dettifoss.
> 10 hours or so from Westman Isles.
> Friday about 1. 30. P.M.

Oh—oh—oh! What a "riotous trip" as the little American who strayed into our 2^d class midst, because there was no other room for her on the boat says! What fun we've got out of it. She & I are the only two women going 2^d. Our companions are:—four Icelanders home for holidays after living in Germany mostly in Hamburg; one nice blue-eyed German from Berlin who can speak French (he & I converse in that—I used Danish for Guðbrandur the steward at first & Mrs Loeb the American uses German!); two Britishers one Macdonald a red-faced, blue-eyed, square-jawed, but humorous ex-engineer from "Bookston", he's been to Australia & this is his 2^d trip to Iceland. His hobby is wild birds & he's going to lake Mývatn in the north to see some. And Mr Moffat about whom more anon. Then Mrs Loeb the American—divorced, who's a dear. She's little & dark & vivacious. Jewish to her somewhere—accustomed to everything it's possible for a wealthy young American to have—(her father built the 2^d biggest suspension bridge in the States) but splendid in her way of accepting everything here—smells (oil and a slight fishiness and paint & turpentine just next door to our eating-place, and other things. We rocked over our bunks to-day. She'd been complaining about hers and I got her to feel my mattress—and she said I ought to send in a bill to the company charging so much per bruise! But I explained I'd discovered how to arrange myself round the worst lump in the straw. Do you remember the worse of the two beds in Mrs Joyner's? Well, it's like that only much more so! And Wednesday was awful—the Dettifoss is 2000 tons, but she doth pitch and she do particularly [love] to perform ye figure of eight. But one gets used to it. And then came fog, thick fog—and it got calmer, hurrah. I lost all I'd eaten all Wednesday but kept stuffing myself with white bread & potatoes & that helped. Then Wednesday night I slept eight hours lumps and all and Thursday was glorious. Almost everyone got up and we walked about enjoying the waves and I almost ate two eggs! And what do you think. Into our eating-room, a rectangular box about 20 feet sq off which four 2 bunk cabins open—(the door has a way of bursting open at akkerd moments whiles)—came two Icelandic girls and one was—Lea Eggertsdóttir whom I met at a tea-party in St Andrews Hall, Reading over two years ago! I remembered her name at once and then off we went to the 1st class smoking saloon and talked and talked. And I'd talked Icelandic with the steward and with a painter doing the side of the ship so we got on famously. I think I'll be able to understand it O.K. up there and it's been grand practice. But at table it's always English. Old Moffat of Lancashire, who's taking his 1st sea-trip ever (never been on a boat before tho' he's helped build hundreds. He's a joiner now. Haddon Hall estate in Derbyshire) is the patriarch of his company. And I call little Elinor Loeb Mother Superior and Chairman etc: etc: she distributes candies after dinner, and keeps us in fits of laughter. She had a special tea-party thrown for her in the House of Commons meeting Sir Philip Sassoon etc: and is about to get engaged to—but I musn't say whom ∵ it hasn't quite come off yet. Her comments are priceless, oh and I was almost forgetting No 11—Mr Ross who is courier to a Mrs B. who's sg to do with the Curtis Publishing C^y. He's from Scotland originally tho' quite Americanised and is a rare hand at telling stories. And I've heard more about the private affairs of the present Majesty of England than ever in me life before—My wig! Though I suspect we can take it with a pinch or two of salt. Also about various other folks whose names mean still less to a body like meself. Old Moffat goes about in a state of dreamy beatitude murmuring how much he's enjoying every minute and wondering why he's never taken a holiday before. He reminds me a bit of Mr Langley if he'd been born "a working man" as Moffat labels himself. And what discussions we've had—about politics, war, religion, birth-control—all taking an active, intelligent part. Little Loeb is a fine chairman—how true it is that folk, who're used to living in what is known as the highest circles of society, if they are intelligent and interested in their kind, can move in every circle with perfect ease & set their fellows at ease. We feel one community and I'm certain our talk is more interesting than the 1st class. As far as I could make out they were comparing cocktails up there! And how that old Lancashire fellow can tell stories. He's tallish and a bit bent with whitish hair, a big nose and humorous shrewd face. And this morning I was up again in the 1st smoking-room with Lea & her friend & the captain joined in and 1st mate. Little Guðbrandur our 2^d cl. steward is a dear—twenty years old and inclined to be stoutish, he'd be a grand wee butler and he's looked after his two women passengers well. He even came in and washed our cabin floor before we got up this morning! Good soft soap they use on board! Now the Icelandic lads are playing quoits & I have "namore to seye" at the moment so— They say we're in for a storm to-night, but that won't matter so much now, since we're almost there—only 30 hours more or so! I am glad tho' that we didn't have to lie flat all the 5 days! We don't get in till Saturday evening! I still feel this is all very dream-like especially after meeting Lea but it is being a gorgeous one. And the sea-air is that restoring. I think I'd have been alright on Wednesday if I'd not been so tired before coming on board. And I did stagger up in between times so it's been simply splendid. Now the drizzle will make what I've written run so I'll walk round a bit. I feel in my bones I'm going to love Iceland just as much as I thought I should! It's getting gey grey now spex we will have it worser again to-night but it's been amazingly calm—no whales as yet.

The G.P.O. Reykjavík. Saturday. 1. 30 P.M.

Just scribbling this while waiting for the car to come & take us out to Thingvellir the Assembly place—it's hot, hot, gorgeous weather—clear mountains & I've had a lunch of salmon & gooseberry porridge with a delightful chimney-sweep & his family Astrid got to know! Oh, my wig how I love Iceland. And old Moffat & young Macdonald & Mrs Loeb & Astrid & I are all going out together. I'll tell you about yesterday when we had a swell storm—swells later—it was so rough they cdn't get in to the harbour & a thick fog & cold as the North Pole the boat rocking so that we almost—just then we decided not to go till 2. 30. P.M. so here are Astrid & I sitting on a hillside overlooking the harbour & Eskja a great flat Table Mountain. There are now five of us—oh but I told you that. I found Old Man Moffat in a Soda Fountain Café enjoying smoked salmon & tea—he'd asked for tea bread-&-butter & cakes & asked me what he'd got! And when he heard the trip to Thingvellir would cost just about 10/- each he leaped at it—he'd thought it'd be £2.15 each when he refused before! Well, about last night, since there is time. We certainly did run into rough weather. First it rained, & then Dettifoss began to plunge and roll but it was glorious and I just revelled in being able to watch it all happening without turning a hair nay rather eating cake & sweet biscuits & drinking tea. The best thing about Dettifoss is that there is so little vibration—I've never been on a quieter boat. I can see her lying quietly in harbour now. And later—fog & a terrific Atlantic swell—my wig how she rolled but some of us stood right up in front looking out for the Westman Isles. And suddenly—a long line of foam about thirty feet high & a sharp edge through grey mist & the ship wheeled almost swerved right round—and we got as near to the harbour entrance as we could. The motor boat—big 'un that came out to meet us looked like a cork on that swell—I don't know how they got to us at all. Then a barge with two blue overalled men who took 12 tons of flour & potatoes into it. And long after—another tug bigger trailing a punt with about thirty passengers *plus* baggage in it—men, women & children & tossing like a bigger cork. How sick some were & when they did get alongside it was too rough to get em on board any other way than by lowering a great round basket about 3 ft across 5 ft high with a door in the side down to their boat & hauling 'em up like baggage—three & four at a time! They swung in a parlous fashion often & my heart was in my mouth for the children. And the poor things were some of 'em just sick on deck as soon as they got there. Old Man Moffat said it was seeing "life in the raw" & it was. Some passed the night in our dining-room lying on stores & the one bit of couch that there is there. But we crawled into our bunks frozen through—we'd had nowt since 6. p.m. and it was 12. 30 before we turned in, and I felt holler as I'd not had a big supper because 6 is so soon after 4. Well—about 6. am. I was up to find the fog had lifted & a strong wind blowing & Iceland's mountains showing clear (like Norway). We even saw Snæfellsnessjökul about 60 miles I think it is north a fine round cone snow-covered. And how delicious an egg & bread & marmalade tasted. Old Man Moffat ate half a loaf almost! And in next to no time it seemed we were in—I had a few mins. talk with some women who'd got on the night before. Then customs officials and then Astrid standing there waving. And much talk about how we'd spend this afternoon on the quay & then a dash for lunch at Astrid's chimney-sweep's, a delightful man with two wee bairns—and such salmon! Just plain boiled the way we had it in Norway with butter & boiled potatoes. Followed by gooseberry porridge & milk. And fresh milk not tinned was good to taste. But the food & especially the accommodation on *Dettifoss* is I think simply excellent. They let you sleep on board too, but I'm coming ashore with baggage to be with Astrid in the nice house she's borrowed from her Swedish friend who's married to an Icelander. We'll fetch luggage after coming back from Thingvellir. They're cutting the grass here with scythes to get the hay & taking it away in little wooden carts like this

The basket they used for passengers last night was like this:-

& they swung it up forty feet & more! Now it's getting all misty again & cooler but I do hope it'll be clear out at Thingvellir. I foresee that the oilskins'l be useful. I used the coat on the way here. This is glorious. Here till Wednesday & then to Akureyri. Muchest love to you all.

Jean
Astrid sends her love.

Johanna & Ingi at Þorsmörk

II

Reykjavik. 7. 7. 36.

Where does the time go to? Here it's the end of the fourth day in Reykjavik and I don't seem to have done anything—except of course seen Thingvellir and Gullfoss & Geysir on Sunday and people yesterday & to-day & walked much about uneven streets strewn with ashes and sand & grit all grey and with pot-holes larger even than the Athenian ones! Well, after Saturday came Sunday—rather cooler but little rain only and the scenery on the 160 mile odd drive was magnificent—Hekla and other snow capped giants in the distance and peak after peak, mile after mile, and terrific swoops down and up in the car. How they ever drive along these "roads" beats me—they're just roughish cart-tracks with tremendous ruts in them over the lava and whiles the bumps even in a luxuriously sprung saloon like the one we were in (we went bust over these two days) were "some" bumps. Mrs Loeb & Mr Moffat & Astrid & the guide Jón Gizurarson and the driver Helgi and I that day. There's iron in the hills—they're light red in places and a queer yellow in others—the dolorite forms itself into octagonal columns here—and here only in the world apparently. Gullfoss simply took our breath away. It's a colossal creature that roars downwards in four distinct falls one broad t'other you can't quite see almost at right angles, then a little drop and then a Niagara like sheer fall into a narrow gorge. The spray is like smoke—you can see it miles away and you hear the roar too. Mrs Loeb said it was better than Niagara because unspoiled—noone there but ourselves! And also no railing to prevent folk from throwing themselves in. It was a pity there was no sun because the rainbows are rather glorious but I liked its white thunder better than any floating colours. What a country. And a beautiful, brilliant tiny heather grows over the lava in little clumps, and there are Swiss flowers one like a white rose too. I wish I knew 'em. And the Iceland gull is such a beautiful creature too—he hovers over the lake down in the town—with delicate long pointed wings and an odd way of fluttering. And we passed old farms—built in the old way of turf & stone and corrugated iron:— It's the space and silence that are so marvel- lous here. On the way back from Gullfoss we visited Geysir, Stóra Geysir (the Big Geysir). We'd had a pastry-cake and cup of tea for breakfast since the start was to have been early 8. 30—actually we waited half an hour for Mrs L. (who'd been plied too much with good drink the night before by the ex-Premier!) and when we got to Geysir it was after 2. But we didn't dare have our meal—at the hotel—in case he spouted. They threw in about 100 lbs or so of soap to encourage him—yellow & pink & the queerest looking white stuff. But he just quietly absorbed it "lay low & said nuffin". But he gradually grew hotter—80°—81°—82°—83° (Celsius) right up to 90—nothing happened. He'd done it on Sunday and he didn't do it for the King of Denmark the other week so—we waited. And the stone (?) round about grew too hot to sit on with comfort—& the steam blew hotter but nothing happened. It rained a little and the distant mountains turned blue-er and nothing happened. And the "crowd" (about fifty or sixty all told) sat or lay or stood chattering. Some had been there from 10. a.m.! At 5. p.m. our insides could hold out no longer—even the Icelandic driver said he was "svangur" (hungry) so we went down to the hotel about five minutes further down the way to eat. My wig how good that tasted—we had two helps of soup, the meat (excellent mutton) and coffee I even got two apricots (tinned) as dessert! And—just as we had finished Helgi saw folk stirring up at the crater I want to call it—it was just like one in miniature—& we tore up in the car wild with excitement. There was Geysir tossing himself about now one way and now another so that boiling soapy water poured down for hundreds of yards from the sides of the "crater". And just as Astrid said "Now it's all over" shot up a column—they said afterwards it was almost 200 feet high (65 metres)—one of the best spouts that's ever been. It was astounding— everyone just yelled with pure thrill—the noise was deafening and it was too exciting for anyone to feel afraid. Imagine it—white & scalding agin a grey sky. And after that steam—steam—steam— steam drifting away up the hillside—red—brown. We lay back in the car a trifle exhausted after both those things. And it had rained heavily nearer Reykjavik so that the colour of the grass and contrasting lava and mountains was a joy—a queer yellow-green and grey-brown and indigo—it's impossible to describe. Iceland is very like Greece except that it's warmer in Greece and the air there is still clearer—at least round about here there's so much dampness that you don't get that crystal clarity of atmosphere. Then, Monday—we walked about the place, meeting Mrs Loeb & Mr Moffat, & we helped him buy a collar & shirt-front & tie to grace the dinner at the hotel with Mrs Loeb. And so to the Museum where a charming little old lady in the national dress simply because I spoke a little Icelandic asked me to come & see her when I returned to Reykjavik! And I learned today that she's a character and a great friend of Professor Sigurd Nordal. She's an assistant curator in the Museum. Then— dinner with Mrs L. It was a pity we had to have it upstairs because Mr Moffat would have so much enjoyed being in the great hall but there was a feast on at 9. 30. for the Swedish Choir that has been over here for the Swedish week. We went to the grounds of a big elementary school (one of the two they have) to hear 'em afterwards & that was good. They do sing superbly. And it was all grey in the distance mist over mountains beyond the sea just over the school-wall and the ugly waste place beyond. They're always building here & much of the town is just hideous—all corrugated iron and stress-concrete— & dusty streets with no pavements strewn with building material, poles, stones which are left lying about even in the main ones. But the shops contain the most up to-date articles & the smart folk here are smarter than I've seen 'em anywhere else. To-day—losh but I was tired—& slept like a stone as they say here from 1. till 9. a.m. It's tiring to hear all the talk & to switch off & on from three languages all day!—we got up late & then I called on Ragnheiður Kjartansdóttir and invited her to coffee with me at the Hotel Borg (the rendez-vous of Reykjavik). Then a lunch of raw carrot (I must get some vegetable I thought!) and lemon-juice & white bread so hard that it was as good as a rusk! Then out to see Sigurd Nordal & a talk with him in English, and then to H.B. for coffee & sublime cream cakes like the Oslo ones tell Madge. By the way Benedikt our host here (whose wife & child are in Sweden) is so like Egil but better-looking & more charming even! And younger! I'm sure he has Irish blood in him—Then a walk round & so home to supper—milk & raisins & a pastry-thing. But we're going to have eggs & tea at midnight. It's never dark now—you can read all through the night. Still feel I'm in a dream—we go to Akureyri to-morrow evening & I want to catch Brúarfoss with this to-night—she sails for Leith at 10. P.M. so I've just time to rush down with it. We're in Akureyri until the end of the month probably. I'll send an address from there. Heaps of love. Jean.

III

S.S. Dettifoss Friday 10th July.
In Ísafjörður, about 1. p.m.

Well—when did I last say aught. My wig I wish you could see this boat—There are G.O.K. how over 500 of us on board—in the holds, on the deck amongst the paraffin casks, timber, sacks of potatoes, furniture, (a whopping big cupboard almost blocks the way in to our 2^d cl. eating-room (note how Icelandic that English translation is!), bad fish etc: Yes, there is a big cask of bad fish on board—it's to go back to the man who palmed it off on folk in Reykjavik! But the fish rotting in the harbour at Patreksfjörður stank so that this solitary cask is as nothing. It's very like Norway at this moment—the west fiords are—but mist on the top of the mountains and snow spattered over the sides down to the water's edge whiles. We're two days late already and don't get to Akureyri till some time on Sunday—we were due there to-day! What happened was that we ran into thick sea-fog on Wednesday night or early Thursday morning & just lay or moved an inch at a time till we got to the first harbour, Patreksfiord. Wednesday was a good day in Reykjavik. I saw professor Guðmundur Finnbogason after we'd been to Einar Jónsson's Museum—he's Iceland's most famous sculptor. I'd only seen photographs of his work before—some of it is very fine tho' not up to Vigeland's, the Norwegian I feel. It was good to see the American's statue of Leif Ericsson standing out agin' the blue mountain over the sea when we came out of the Museum. And then Ásgrim Sveinson's—his studio is in his house. I liked his "Viking" much, also "Boy and Girl" (title taken from the first Icelandic novel written the middle of last century). Then we drank coffee with the nice chimney-sweep Thorkel again—we'd had dinner there before. And then to Guðmund F. where we got more coffee! He has a garden with pansies in it and lupins & it was pleasant to sit in the sun there a few minutes. The weather was the best we've yet had that day. To-day it was warm ashore but I've got on everything I can put on at the moment. We're sitting right up in the bows—the beak comes up high & it's out of the wind we're sitting on the trap-door over the anchor. Well, after leaving Guðmund we went to a friend of Sigfus's (as I can now call Dr Blöndal in Icelandic!) who gave us a goodly supper! "Kvæfi" a sort of potted sheep-sausage—meat v. good, and eggs & smoked salmon slices, and marmalade & biscuits & tea. After which Astrid and I decided we'd only need one meal a day on the ship! Here, after Reykjavik you pay

2kr per meal & don't have to pay whether you eat or not as before. So we laid in a store of standard bread, dried fish (cod) (you just tear bits off & eat it, dried apricots & prunes & chocolate. And the sunset over the hills opposite the harbour was a joy. It was glorious. We didn't leave till midnight and retired before we sailed. The next day—fog, thick, cold drifting about shutting out everything. And for hours & hours & hours we just lay or moved inch-wise. We watched great jelly-fish with ribbon-like streamers floating by, lilac and orange and green looming curiously through the pale grey water. Everything was pale & grey and a wintry sun tried to struggle through. One of the Reykjavik girls produced an accordion like the one Eileen Whitwell brought back from Germany & they danced two or three. What a crowd came on at Reykjavik to travel III. They're most of 'em down in the hold with the cargo—And what a shindy the first night. Poor Mr Moffat couldn't sleep because 4 raided his cabin (they have no keys) with a bottle of whisky 2 men & 2 girls & they drank themselves blind drunk until 2. a.m. We heard 'em but they didn't come in to us. Anyway there was so much noise elsewhere it didn't make much odds. How I wish Mrs Loeb could have seen life on this boat. I think I'm the only English body on board. Most are Icelanders. The girls from Reykjavik and indeed everywhere wear long grey flannels & 'd look very nice—they're far more becoming than shorts—if only they didn't wear the highest of high heels and town hats and bags (hand-bags) and town coats with them! Patent high-heeled shoes! And they use too much make-up. The country lasses on the other hand are extraordinarily beautiful some of them—lovely eyes and glorious clear skins and glowing. It was very funny—oh but I told you about the remark the American tourist made about Astrid & myself who are a fine brown and red at the moment, didn't I? She thought we were Icelanders. Well—we drifted all Thursday & about 5. got in to Patreksfjörður—an excellent little fishing-village stretching along a bay. And then they took ashore the little Icelandic pony who'd been on deck all that time. He was good—only couldn't eat or drink at all. And Léa Eggertsdóttir was on board too & we & her sister & a friend walked a mile or two along the shore & I had dried cod and dry bread & apricots & prunes for supper by a running stream where the silver trout were lying half under stones. It was a wild desolate looking place with mist over the heights & nowt but stones, stones, stones over the grass. But it has character that place and I don't wonder that an Irishman called Örlyg elected to settle there his first winter in this country. He went south later. There was a shed where they clean the fish there and another like a factory with a chimney that smoked vilely as we drew in and great tarpaulin covered stacks of fish everywhere along the shore. And another kind, halibut I think hanging up to dry. The Icelanders bought some & walked along chewing it, but I liked my cod from Reykjavik better! Then away again slowly through the fog, and we were invited to Lea's sister's cabin (1st) and we chatted & I played 'em a tune or two on the pipe. So to bed—I couldn't catch a lot of what they said, but enough to understand the subject they were discussing. This morning up early—before 8. that is to find we were in Ísafiord. And ashore with Léa (she's the girl who came to Reading two & a bit years ago) to her sister's home where we got gorgeous hot coffee & cakes & biscuits. Then a walk through the town to the house of an old wood-carver called Guðmundur from Mosdal who showed us his work— horns and boxes & metalwork and other things). Now—we're rocking, pitching slightly so I think I'll stop writing—we're right aft & it's not easy to write straight. Have I my sea-legs I wonder! So long—out in the open sea we are now.

Saturday. 4. 30. p.m.

Ingolfsfiord. Friday. 10. p.m.

And they said we'd be here a short time! The boat came in at 7. 30 or so, and we walked up a mountain & sat by a pleasant little waterfall (I'd call it big in England!) in three bits that came slithering & sliding down. And there was the scent of thyme all round & a mist over the hill higher up. It's blotting out everything but the little fishing station here. There are only three houses here and almost 200 got off here to help with the herring I think. (There must have been over 500 on board that last 2 days) They had tents & bedding with 'em—and great solid boxes with gear. I expect they sleep on the floor in the longest house in rows. Most of the lads have tents—they're putting 'em up now. But it's chiefly girls & women. Besides the three houses of which Ingolfsfiord consists there are:– (1) colossal stacks of barrels as high as a three-storied house they appear to make 'em on the spot I 'spose the timber comes from Reykjavik & there's a lot of drift-wood about too. (2) sheds not yet roofed where they'll wash the fish and the long rectangular wooden sinks they use—they're just standing on the jetty with planks & barrels & timber. (3) clothes lines with fishing garments drying (in the fog.!) (4) one of the three houses isn't yet finished—they're turning in at it now. I think the herring catch was bigger than anticipated also that it was made earlier. I saw summat about it in the papers in Reykjavik. This house underneath has timber, barrels of salt, a huge saw, sacks of stuff, two spinning-wheels, a Napoleonic (time I mean) Empire sofa & a couple of dead sea-gulls that nobody seems to bother about turfing out. I thought the smell came from the fish at first! This is life in the raw but much better-paid & easier than earlier on I 'spose. The lasses have good stout bibs & braces & smoke & sing—some were sea-sick before we turned in here—Astrid & I found Dettifoss pitching a bit much so retired for four hours & really slept. That was glorious and how luxurious did I not feel my straw mattress was—and the good cabin for only two after what I'd seen of the hold where the folk were packed like sardines. And the little dining & smoking-room is really palatial! Old Man Moffat is only delighted that we shan't get to Akureyri until Sunday praps even Monday now. It's all along of the herring we're calling now at so many harbours. But it *is* cold. The fog is drifting about everywhere & I've on not only a woolly (which, thanks be, I stuck in at the last minute!) but my green suède coat and linen overcoat & it's too chilly to sit really. But I wanted to describe this place to you. It's the sort of place their greatest modern author had in mind—Halldor Kiljan Laxness, when he wrote "Salka Valka" a book you should read but remember that it's only the ugliest side of life here that he describes in that book. Oh, it is fun to come this way with the folk themselves & not as a tourist on a tourist boat—even if it does mean spending extra time at sea instead of ashore. The air is glorious—& the pine log I'm sitting on, on the shingle smells good. Guess there are some happy couples amongst the folk—here come two, a fellow in blue jersey & she's in a tweed jacket with a tartan scarf—most of the younger women are in trousers. They're still unloading sacks (of potatoes I expect) and tin barrels of paraffin—besides personal luggage. They were 8 hours loading the *last* day in Reykjavik, so you can just imagine how much they took on board! Astrid gave a huge sniff then so I'll stop & we'll go another walk.

How one eats & sleeps here—we had two helps of the hot course some kind of stewed stuff & potatoes then cold meats & beetroot & cheese & rye-bread & white bread & hot tea. After all it was our first meal since 9. 30. a.m. or so—we only had a slice of bread & two prunes in between! And the Icelandic progresses tho' slowly. I must read some grammar on this boat. I didn't take anything else to read with me—no need with so much to see. An old fellow came riding by on a white horse called Högni (he's a famous person in old poetry) when Astrid & I were walking by the shore after coming down the mountain. It's never dark now—but how I'd love a spot of sun again—it *is* grey, grey & desolate & fishy here!

11. 30. p.m. In our cabin

The latest was that we shouldn't get away to-night but the fog is lifting slightly—a queer salmon streak appeared at the opening of the fiord a few moments ago so—with luck we'll reach Akureyri this Sunday only 3 days late! They're dancing on the jetty here now to a gramophone, & an Icelandic girl who's on holiday from Reykjavik & who's invited me to come & see her there is having a gay time with the brother of the German from Berlin, they're dancing now. I forgot to include in the scrappy picture of this place the river that made the falls & the tubs for washing fleeces in ley, and the new-washed wool hanging out on the wall to dry—the unwashed heaped up down by the water. Now we're warmer & after a dried apricot or so—to bed. Life is good!

Saturday. 4.30. p.m.

Now, this is something like! We almost froze in our bunks last night—after all we're in the Arctic circle & A. & I didn't get up till nearly 11. (& cut breakfast). Ingolfsfiord, no Djúpavík was just two houses & a factory where they made fish-meal (cattle-food). My wig, what smells—cod-liver oil chief but dead fish also & smoke etc: & it *was* cold (no breakfast inside us either). I walked about a bog with the two nice Germans & we talked broken Icelandic to each other—they photographed a waterfall—that came down sheer from a steep precipice above the factory—& forked prettily. Didn't dinner consisting of boiling hot apple-soup followed by chunks of curried mutton rice & potatoes taste good. But how well we all look & feel—the simple life is good. And now, sun, blessed, blessed, blessed sun, warming & streaming and pouring itself and flooding the sea & the mountains and the deck aft where we're sitting—oh it is good not to feel numb & chill any more and the fishing lasses are playing mouth organs & concertinas and I pippled on the pipe a wee while back. This is Steingrimsfiord—in the north—we've turned the N.W. corner now so maybe good-bye to the fog. Anyhow I can't grumble at the weather—no real rain yet & a whole week & more & 1st time A was here she had 2 days out of 6 weeks when she could see beyond her nose! It's even more lovely than the Norwegian fiords I think because you can see so much more, tho' of course they're more impressive. It all reminds me much of that cruise except that it's so much much rougher & wilder & cruder & desolate and full of smells and grubbier! But fish gets companionable I shall miss the smells of this boat when ashore. Now we're coming to Hólmavík, we'll get to Akureyri some time next week?

Siglufjörður. Sunday. 10. 15. p.m.

Hólmavik was pleasant—a breeze blowing from the land & the boats came out to us for their telegraph poles and paraffin & potatoes & metal pipes etc: & Astrid & I had a meal of a slice of brown bread & 6 dried prunes & some dried cod up aft in the sun out of the wind. And there was a good sunset & we sat there asking each other grammatical questions till it got cold. Rougher during the night, more fog & very cold again. To-day I got up about 10 and sat talking with the Germans and Mr Moffat till it got really a bit rough & I had to retire to my cabin for dinner—which I ate however—I'd been so hungry before! Soup & meat & rhubarb porridge & milk. I lay down between the courses &—all was well. Even Astrid the stalwart retired after the rhubarb! At 4. p.m. about we got here—pouf!—do you know what burning herring fat smells like? Add strong cod-liver oil and bad fish to that & you've got the odour of Siglufjörður. But I noticed we got acclimatised after 4 hours on shore. We went to a baker's shop & got bread & milk—*and* glorious, sublime, marvellous ecstasy-giving SKÝR (Icelandic sour milk—thick like ice-cream, with sugar and cream. It beats even the Greek "jaourti" which up till now has been the best variety I've yet sampled. And three Salvation Army lassies stood outside & played on guitars and sang & preached to the folk idling about of a Sunday afternoon. The wind was bitter—so we crouched in a hollow up the mountain-side to look at those opposite—great peaks rising sheer almost as they do in Norway, a rose-brown colour (stones) yet flecked with green at the base and snow lying in great swathes right down to the sea-level sometimes. And mist shrouding their peaks, drifting incessantly in from the sea and just above us—obscuring the sun so that all the little grey corrugated iron or concrete houses looked greyer—here & there a green or red-brown roof. And mound after mound of herring-barrels piled up along the many piers—I counted 15 in one part alone—with the tubs & rectangular troughs & salt-boxes all ready for the 20th when the great work begins. There's only about half-a mile of habitable land here so the houses are tight-packed & the place dominated by chimneys just like the one that emits the yellow smoke Maisie

Letters from Iceland 1936   15

dislikes most in Glossop. Just that colour of smoke, also an evil green-grey & some whiter was being belched forth by these such here. We wandered about four hours or so sts sitting in hollows out of the wind and decided we *wouldn't* like to pass the summer at Siglufjörður but it's not as bad as I thought it'd be nor so large. And what spirit some of the folk have—opposite these giant snow mts and in the teeth of winds that blow straight from the north was a house with a really lovely little garden—grass & all kinds of little stunted shrubs & trees & flowers! And one of the crew came by just after we'd admired it & greeted us & gave us the extra bit the Icelanders tack on if you're related or if they specially like you "blessed"! We felt we'd gone up one. Helgi the taxi-driver did that also—in Reykjavik. A nice young botanist on holiday (a student in Copenhagen) (Icelander) has joined our company in the 2^d & as he's going to C'hagen on Astrid's boat in August that's pleasant. Now, we're aboard again—due to leave some time before midnight we hope—the crane is rumbling furiously just overhead (our cabin I forgot to say is contiguous but we're so sleepy we sleep through everything—I even did through Dettifoss' departing blasts one night! It'll be good to get ashore for a spell after this extra long trip in sea-fog! We ought to have reached Akureyri last Friday! And yet another harbour before we make Akureyri. The Icelanders in the hold almost all of whom came off here—(that is over 450!) were singing "It's a long way to Akureyri" the other evening! It was interesting to see how it could be done—their transportation I mean—you'd never believe it if I wrote it down—but you can imagine what it's meant—there's only accommodation for 12 2^d and I think it's 24–30 (1st class) & the "hold" men & women share what convenience there is! Astrid & I simply had to raid the 1st whiles—& the queue outside our dining-room (off which the cabins open) was difficult to push through! This is a plan of our quarters

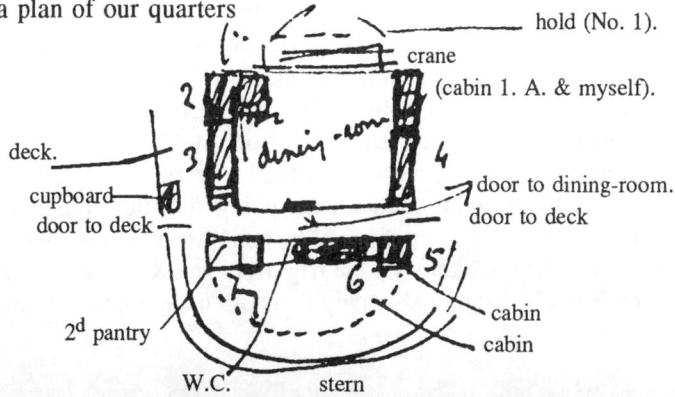

This is more of a cargo boat than passenger really & that's why we've been so long & why it was possible to get all the hold-class on board, amongst the paraffin & sewing-machines & flour & potatoes & beer, and timber and zinc(?) pipes, & chest-lavatories (that's what the huge cupboard they dumped just outside our door was! Well, we may go "Hold" ourselves east from Húsavík to Seyðisfjörður— it all DEPENDS, not with 550 herring-salters for me. I've seen what it's like and that's enough. But goodness what luxurious lives we live in England. We're so far removed from so much. Hop-pickers of course live in pretty much the same way. I wonder if my hard-up women students take on such a job sometimes—I must find out. It's well-paid, they can make if they're quick workers from 25–30/- a day at it—hence the rush to the herring stations during July & August— it only lasts 2 months & what they make then has usually to carry 'em through the whole year. And now—good-night. There's a *cow* on board now, we dropped the horse somewhere—& Astrid thought it was a fog-horn but I knew it was a moo I heard! And the noise continued till next port!

Akureyri. Monday Noon. 13/7/36.

Yes—at last fours nights & 3 days late here we are. All last night that crane rumble-rumbled & casks & bins & poles dumped down at Dalvik—we must have got there about 2. a.m. Arrived here at 6. 30. a.m. & we leapt up hastily & dressed in case anyone should come to meet the boat. But all was well—they'd almost given up hope, having been on the look-out since Friday morning, early. And after lugging our gear up the steep hill wasn't it just good to sit quietly in the delightful little alcove off the living-room where both our beds are. And—there were flowers, lupins (blue) & marguerites in a jug on the table between them! I've seen a garden here too all a-blowing with Californian poppies & lupins & columbines & red daises. And the fields aglow with buttercups. It's grey & coldish but so quiet after that boat—deliciously peaceful. I think the old way of getting about in this country was best—horse-back—M^r McDonald (the other Englishman who came on Dettifoss from Hull) said that several Icelanders were sick all the way in the bus going from here to the Westfirths! We're taking it but are not going to do the whole journey in one day as he did 9. a.m–11. 30. p.m.! He said his head's all bruised yet from the bumps on the frightful roads & one was all along a sheer drop of I forget how many feet. But having travelled by bus in Greece I think I'm hardened. Never shall I forget that night-journey from Megalopolis to Andritseana as long as I live with nice Mr Christ Christopolos at the end to greet us. I think we're going to stay here till Thursday & then once more to sea (there'll only be one little stretch of the island I've not been round then!) in a Norwegian boat *Nova*—where we hope to get 2^d berths for the night—to Seyðisfjörður thence to Hallormstað east. I'm looking forward to that much. They say the weather here has been glorious—almost too hot! Seems funny to think of heat-waves in America & here it's chilly in a suède coat & woolly skirt & all & no wind blowing. But, this is after all *Ice*land. Akureyri is rather lovely—there's a great snow covered mountain called Coldback lying out to sea & it's all lit up by sunlight even though it's grey & misty inland. And snow-streaked others all around, but not so high as to be overwhelming. The snow on the Siglufiord mountains was curiously like animals' tongues lolling down their sides last night. And just before I turned in about midnight the sun was reflected on the topmost peak of one—the highest & all the mist between it & the next—a great white almost fluffy cocoon was suffused a most delicate pink. What a contrast to turn to the reeking chimneys of the little port itself—there were at least eight I discovered after all and one was black. This gets dull but we're both a bit drowsy after that crane-filled night. I may have a swim this afternoon to wake me up tho' they tell me the water's warm from the springs? (Didn't know there were any here). We're staying with another friend of Astrid's—also gymnasticists at least Thorhildur's husband is—he's in Germany now for the Olympic Games—her mother & father live too next story up & her sister's here too & her little girl about 8 & a baby boy of 6 months—a sturdy rogue who looks about a year. Well—don't know what to say about posts—I've not got aught from you yet—but it'll be in Reykjavik again 2^d week in August I spex. Meantime—muchest love to you. This *is* such fun.

J.

2. P.M. Glorious sunshine suddenly & we're going swimming!

IV

Egilsstöðum. Völlum.
July 18. 1936.

Ah-ha said the duck laughing as the sun came out once more at last after almost a fortnight's total absence behind fog and cloud and drizzle. Ain't it hot too in this sitting-room where I've just written to ask Eleanor if she'd care to spend a winter here teaching English to three children in return for skiing skating etc: The good lady of the house asked me if I knew of anyone who'd care to! That's the second time I've been asked summat sich since I came. And all in Icelandic & I had to answer ditto! What fun it all is. Well Akureyri was obstinately shrouded in fog, fog, fog and drizzle, only one afternoon fine when I bathed with the little Ragnhildur Steingrimsdóttir in the open-air bath filled with water from hot springs up in the hills that gleamed snow covered as we swam! So we'll just let A. go by— we read & played (pipe!) & sewed (Astrid did) & once had a blissful short walk over the bog—it's very like Ireland up there only wilder. Then came Thursday & we embarked on Nova a Norwegian boat. Journey bad—visibility nil—comfort not much. I was very sick once— all over the cabin floor alack as they'd not put the bottoms in the containers. So that was uncomfortable. But we got at last to Seyðisfjorður after lying completely still & not being it again for almost 16 hours & the sea just heaving & I slid up & down & down & up (you almost stand on your head & that's a queer feeling but all very interesting & I dried gradually & they mopped up the floor so that was better but my wig the heat—with the heating on & the porthole locked (had to be or the sea'd have flooded us). Well I got up at Seyðisfjorður & we walked a mile or so to ask about buses & such-like & arrange for our gear to come. And after an hour we got blessed tea (so weak that even I could have done with stronger) & bread & sausage bright-red with white spots & very strong tasting and scented, & cheese. And behold that was very good and the giddiness began to pass away and I to contemplate a 24 km tramp over the mountains with joy. A nice lad let us change stockings & re-arrange our kit in his shop and promised to put the rucksacks etc: on the car when it came (you never know when it will here!) & off we set with literally only tooth-brushes & some bread & chocolate in our pockets—over the mountains. And the sun came out (it grew foggy only towards evening) & there were rainbows dancing in the most glorious falls I've ever seen—at least ten roaring giants all close on 80 feet high and 40 ft broad! Some forked and some opposite each other—and roaring so you couldn't hear a word. That's characteristic of this land—the sound of fiercely rushing water. And up & up & up to the snow-line & beyond, are rivers we had to wade (no bridge nor nothing & I understand now why Icelanders never *walk*!) & then to a desolate "heath"—all stones & snow & water & more water & snow & stones for mile after mile.

Next Monday. 11.15. a.m.

Well, I didn't get much written last time—where I left off on Saturday Astrid's friend Unnur came to tell us that coffee & *horses* were ready! So we drank coffee—for 3^d time that day (we had our "meal" at 8. P.M. when we arrived here, Hallormstað—and donned various trousers & I was lent nailed & spiked mountain boots & off we set at a fine canter for—almost 4 hours! Well, during the first 20 mins I held tight on to Hákur's mane (as told to) because we really were riding at a good pace—I've never ridden so fast before—& only tried "the canter" just last lesson. And then I got such a stitch in the right side I thought I'd burst and I felt it'd be impossible to endure another five minutes let alone over three hours. But we varied the pace—the "trot" is like Chinese torture to begin with! you don't rise in the stirrups the horse is too small you just *bump*! Well I bumped they bumped we bumped but Hákur was worst—even Unnur said he was a bad 'un ("*vondur*") but I got into the way of kicking him with all me legs & he cantered instead & it's far less painful to the seat. After an hour we paused & I found I'd got second wind and simply loved the rest of the journey. Now on the "road" (rough stone track) but now through grassy bogland splish splash, now up the mountainside over the lava, now over road again, now on the rough grass alongside and always the huge, milky river below and in the distance snow hills and the most glorious deep blues indigoes & purples in the evening light. All colour comes from the hills—there's no heather, just little single clumps of sweet-smelling thyme. Well, we rode on & on & I never knew it'd be as glorious as it was—Hákur tried to walk home once or twice but in the end he just obeyed. He was really very good with a beginner & a "furriner" at that I think. It's been a test of riding—walking up a hill is easy enough—it's this cantering along the hard highway that tells. Then we got right down to the river—and little birch-trees began suddenly to appear on our left—it is refreshing to see a wee tree just higher than yourself and bluebells (Scotch) below in the grass—and buttercups & clover and red sorrel and a good smell. And on & on & up a little & so to Hallormstað. And then a "meal"—cold smoked meat and sausage and egg and herring—& onion & rye bread & spinach sauce & radishes & lettuce (!) and tea & biscuits & jam. I enlarge because we were that hungry having ridden and all on three coffees & some bits of cake & biscuit all day. It's like that here—now little now superabundance. I grow fat here I fear. Well, we retired—we've a room called Þverá (= Cross River) after a big river in the south—Hallormstað is a weaving-school and domestic science place in the winter-months and a Guest House in the summer. It's run by relations of Dr Blöndal.—Benedikt & Sígrun. She is large and kindly and we like both of 'em much. It's a new building and blessed with indoor sanitation—"it" was in the cow-shed at Egilsstað but nice & clean & warm & sweet-smelling along of the cows' breath—tho' draughty—the depths were so deep down below! I must tell you about the good lady at Egilsstað. I wrote about Elinor of course, and before we departed à cheval we asked for our bill. And she said there wasn't any for either of us because I was taking that trouble for her about finding someone to go there for the winter or to be "exchanged"! So Astrid gave her a little Swedish brass cigarette ash tray from Uppsala and we parted on excellent terms (as they say in the Sagas). I'm going to have a busy time thinking of presents when I come home—I've paid nothing for staying here at all yet and it looks rather as though I won't all the time I'm here! And I'm seeing North, South, East & West and have been almost all round the island. I weeded once at Akureyri and promised to help a girl there to come to England and here I make hay (when the sun shines as it has done *once* so far) and Astrid weaves. Well to go back to this place. It is large & roomy & our room is nice with two little beds & a third along t'other wall, pale green distemper & white window & brown door & board floor. And great feather eiderdowns as our only covering—feathers not down this time. And I rejoice—it's that *cold* here. At Akureyri the window wouldn't open and it didn't matter so now you know how chilly it is here. There's a big hall downstairs where they burn birch-twigs of an evening if guests arrive & a study lined with books where we sit sewing & darning, a dining-room and a lovely warm kitchen, blue paint & white, where we have meals unless "guests" come. Astrid & I count as part of the household which is most pleasant. We all eat together 'cept some of the men who seem to be out in the fields all day. And we shake hands & thank after every meal just as we did in Norway. Sunday was chill—mist & fog & we never put our noses outside (I did at bed-time through the window only!) but read & chatted & darned. People come in cars occasionally—and get fed & depart. Yesterday was better—rain in the morning a little but later sun though the north wind was icy. Imagine *me* going out on 15 mile tramp over the mountains in not only a jumper (blue, not woolly) but green suède coat AND great heavy double-lined oilskin jacket & NOT being too hot! And I *rode* thus on Saturday evening & at home I wear only a short sleeved jumper & am too hot so! But this is Iceland. And the folk here say it's "exceptional" weather (like our spring *was*). Well, yesterday after 1. (we dine at 12.) I set off on a grand solitary tramp & went miles—the blue snowcapped giants lured me on and on they looked so near & I did get up high & had a magnificent view over Lagarfljot. It is lovely country here—and lonely. I met no-one—only sheep & three kinds of wild bird I didn't know—long-legged with long yellow bills & a curious cry, & a habit of following you "gói" they're called here, and ravens. Two circled above screaming when I lay down under a rock once. And only the sound of running water from the multitudinous streams. There's a big one here—that makes waterfalls just alongside the house—we splashed through on our way here on Saturday. Well—I got back over bog, and lava and mountain & rock & through the little birch-wood time for supper about 7. 15. and then darned some socks for Frú Sígrun Blöndal Herr Benedikt's & her son's. Then to bed. Up to-day at 6. 45. as Fru. B. & a girl who was staying here were off on a 4 day tour up to Dettifoss & back. Then I washed—down in the grand big washhouse in the cellar—birch-twigs under a huge copper & now pyjamas & vest & breeks & stockings & socks & towel & handkerchief flap gaily in the north wind. And while I washed I had a grand chat with a little German woman Frøken Weiner who's a great friend of Léa Eggertsdóttir's sister's—the one who gave us coffee in Ísafjörður. (Iceland's like that they all seem to know each other). She's interesting. Like many folk—women—here she didn't want a house & home—was a wander-bird but wanted a child so just had one and is now bringing him up here. She went back to Germany once but couldn't bear it after the free life here & decided to stay for ever. And she'd rather Isleifur (who's two, almost) grew up a farmer here than be clapped into uniform & sent out to be gassed or shot. Really

Europe seems one horrible nightmare from this distance. People are poor here and life is hard & very primitive in many ways but they *live* and don't look forward to war as inevitable. How sane it all feels here and natural and kindly & sensible. It's good to be here for a bit. The illegitimate child counts as much as one from married parents here & there is absolutely no stigma attaching to either mother or child and a number of, professional women, especially have a child thus. I'd heard it was so, years ago, but had never personally met anyone who'd profited by the law here thus. She's a cheerful little body & says it's simply splendid to have Isleifur and makes all the difference to work & life. She was living with Léa Eggertsdóttir's sister, when Isleifur was born. I liked that sister—she seemed to have much character. Well, well, imagine all that talk & exchange of ideas between a German & an Englishwoman over wash-tubs in a cellar in Iceland! And after, we had coffee—an extra "sup" up in the kitchen and hung our washing out to blow. Then I made hay—turned over the cocks to air & dry—but there's little to do yet so I'm scribbling to you instead. They say they're going to cart the hay after dinner (it's just on 12. now). One thing I've noticed about Icelanders—they use the word "gaman" so much. It seems to mean our "fun". Everything tends to be "fun" here—washing, and hay-making, and everyday work as well as travelling about. Enough for the time being ...

Wednesday. 9. 30. P.M.

It must have been Tuesday yesterday. There's the loveliest light on that broad milky river now & Snæfell the 2^d highest mt. in Iceland is blue like blue ink (or paper) & white up the dale to the south & there's just the sound of the stream all the time and the wind. There was a shower to-day so I read a saga (about this part of the country) until it was dry enough to weed & turn hay. My wig! How fast they work. I lay flat when I came in before supper—but I kept up. They just do it without thinking & I find the left-handed up-hill right to left difficilé. And it's up & down & bunny-holes (or fox'es) and bumps & rocks! And how good dinner at 11. 30. a.m. tasted—chunks of salted mutton with swedes and a plate of hot lentil soup. Followed by coffee. Then real coffee (= tea) at 3. P.M. More work and supper— raw herring & onion & potatoes and again cold porridge mixed with sour milk! And cheese & rye-bread & thin slices of sausage. Sorry to enlarge on food thus but it is interesting these days in more ways than one. It's excellent here and plenty of it and coffee going all day almost. I'm sorry Astrid doesn't like it. Eleanor wd enjoy being here. Have I described the place? Snæfell far in the distance up the dale to the south (house faces west) beyond "heath" (i.e. grass and rocks & lava & mountainy pasture) and "the wood" to the north climbing up the hills behind the house. And the stream rushing down on the Snæfell side & the tún (grass meadow) stretching down towards the huge river (a good few hundred yards away and down & heath-hills like a great down stretching away opposite. Now Astrid & I hop out for 5 mins (she weaves all day) before bed. How sleepy I be.

Sunday. 11. a.m.

Well, since Wednesday—hay-making—phew! Thursday was good some hot sun as well as cool southerly wind blowing & we were at it until *11. 30. p.m.* almost! Because rain had been forecast! And as well as the sour milk-&-porridge meal we got "hlummur" little pancakes & jam with coffee at nearly midnight before retiring—and all in the dim twilight, that comes these evenings at that hour, in the big warm kitchen. It was a glorious evening too. Up the dale rose Snæfell blue and white but with rose-flushed swathes of cloud half-way up, and then deep indigo hills nearer and opposite the afterglow of sunset—it goes down behind the hills so you don't get the sun itself at the end. And above us t'other side the mountain all gold in the reflected light. Then twilight & nowt but the scrape—scrape—scrape of the steel rakes in the stubble. It's gloriously rhythmical once you get into it. But how I ached that night—all over! We did $3^1/_2$ hours on end between 7. 45 and 11. 15! Then Friday was cold—the wind changed to north betokening alack rain so we lammed in at getting the last field (now mown—more to come) finished. When I say "field" I mean bit of moorland by a rushing stream & as up & down & bumpy & stony whiles as may be! And lateish that night too. And before the evening meal this time hot coffee drunk in the lea of a stack—the north wind was icy! It's so comic to make hay with your nose running as fast as it does ski-ing! And I'm learning the technique (Icelandic) of blowing it without a handkerchief! Then Saturday (yesterday) binding into "*baggar*" great bundles it takes two stout fellows (men or women) to heave onto a low long hay-cart (*grind*). You gather huge armfuls & fling it onto a rope consisting of two hand-woven wool strands (Shetland wool colour & most beautiful to behold) ending in two tent-peg affairs with holes. The loose ends are put through the holes round the hay & then tugged as hard as may be—usually a man does that while a girl hangs on to t'other side of the hay-bundle which is often pulled right over (with her on top) on to the man. They have huge fun—I "bound" thus with each of the girls who were out that day. But mostly I just lugged armfuls and put the ropes through the pegs. e.g.

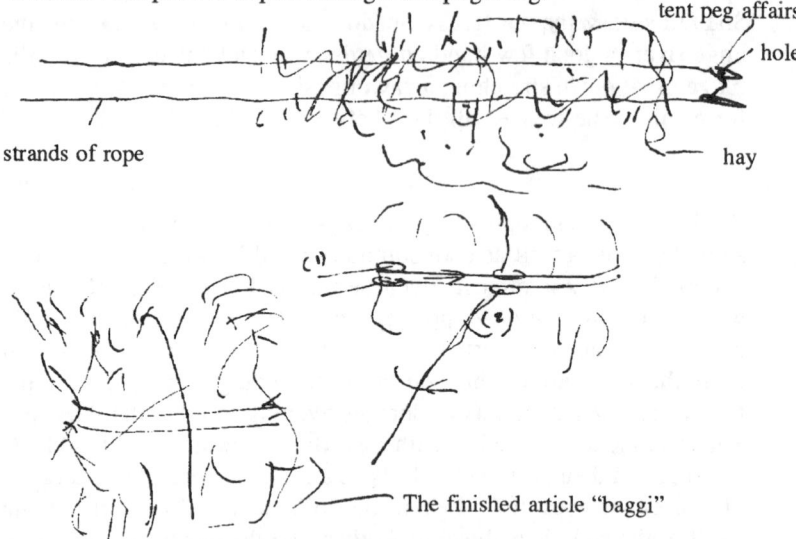

That was yesterday—also I dried up much—took 1½ hours after supper *alone*! There came many guests—about twelve or fourteen in a "*bill*" (car). How I admire the girls who work here. There are four—Ingunn she's a great hefty strong one who helps the heftiest man to bind the "baggar". Very sun-burned (more peony than I am—much—I'm brownish (from the wind chiefly) now & dark-haired—chestnut light in it. Wears a skirt brown & blouse which as she says are allus parting company—she calls it "*detta í sundr*" = "coming to bits". Then two sisters Guðrun and Birna (pronounced Bidd-na) little slight lassies both unco' pretty first fair, wears often a crimson & grey woolly jumper & blue-wool woven skirt. Birna is dark & slight usually in her black dress & cap & apron (she's the parlour-maid when guests come) otherwise in a longish blue-flecked with flowers frock that looks well against the green grass. Then last but by no means least Anna in the kitchen. She's only 21, but tossed off a dinner for 100 guests the other Sunday when Stauning (Premier of Denmark) was here. We saw him in his car on our way riding here from Egilsstoðum & waved to him. She's a rare cook—the food here is just excellent. Only fault so good that you eat more than you need. But how ravenous does field-work make you—worse than walking. I eat four times what I do at Reading! Egg & cheese & jam breakfast milk & coffee. Then a two-course dinner at midday. Afternoon coffee with bread & cheese & little buns. The supper (cold meat, cheese, salad, herring) sts a cup of coffee before bed. Terrific. Anna is big & fair (rather like Maisie sometimes I think—only grey-blue eyes instead of deep blue). And a very nice lass. Never put out just walks away with sleeves rolled up, smiling, saying little but always ready tho' sts a bit late with the household's meals if guests arrive in large numbers unexpectedly as they sts do. And I've acquired the Icelandic technique of drying up with a *wet* dish-cloth! You simply wring it out (it's soaking after two or three great ashets) & go on using it, and as the things come out of boiling water it answers! I was a bit amazed when after asking her what I'd use, she (Anna) took the soaking cloth, popped it into the boiling water & wrung it out & handed it to me. Then I darned socks (Hr Blöndal's) last night. To-day is Sunday & Astrid is darning (she's been weaving all the time till now) & I'm scribbling this & now going to read before "*middegisverð*". How these lassies work. After all that hay-making & cooking & washing-up & cleaning they bake bread & wash! Often get about 4–5 hours in bed only! And the men work too. Hr. Blöndal and his 11 year old son Siggi (Sigurðr) with them. He doesn't go to school—there isn't one anywhere near here—what happens is that an itinerary teacher who tries to cope with all subjects & all ages comes to a neighbouring farm (praps twenty miles off) & stays there a bit & children come & live there for some weeks to learn—But then folk say they can teach Siggi as much as these teachers do & in better conditions so he's here at home. Many of Iceland's most famous modern writers never had a day's "schooling" in their lives—just read at home. Siggi is red-haired & terrifically freckled & bright blue eyes smile at you from the freckles. Then there's A.B.C! The name (pronounced "*ah bay say*") that two-year-old Isleifur (the German girl's son) gave him. He's burned & red-tow coloured tousled hair—a bit bowed tho' he's very young, from scything the grass & carting much. Then Skúli the foster-son of the Blöndals, dark-haired, dark-eyed and with a funny little giggle that many Icelandic men seem to be born with. The women laugh but the men giggle. He's always chewing straws. ABC. whose real name is Hrafn (Raven) smokes a lot, pipe & cigarettes but he's the only person of this entire household who does (pen ran out) Now lastly Odd. who comes sts—I like him light brownish hair sun-burned & a good smile. And old Einar Long, proud of his English ancestry. He carves, draws, (self-taught) & makes up poetry & drinks much coffee also stronger stuff. Haven't seen much of him but he helped Astrid with a tool she wanted for weaving & I saw one of his designs (for embroidery) & it was remarkably good. He sits up of nights doing 'em he says. Now for a read—Independent Folk (about Iceland) by Halldor Kiljan Laxness the author of *Salka Valka* a book you ought to read (Laxnes)

Tuesday 11. 15 a.m.

Well—what a hoot. Yesterday it continued to rain a little. Sunday a downpour but I went out with a pleasant school ma'am from Akureyri (lent her my rucksack & carried her handful of gear for her) & her friend to see the former off over the *flot* (river) in a boat which they plugged with a whiskey-cork before setting out! And well it was I donned me oilskins! I was wading up over the knees in some "swollen" streams—quite difficult to keep one's footing in some but not a drop came through—only a slight dampness in one stocking. Good for what's their name in Croydon—Millett's. It was fun too coming back because the farmer who accompanied the man intending to move her over had a horse with him & when he heard we'd gone just to see her off (& the water streaming everywhere & mist) he just said "Now I am surprised" (a literal translation of his Icelandic & it was the way he said hissa (surprised) that was so funny, &—let us ride in turns all the way back! I nipped up the hill with him first, phew I was hot—but it's a comfort to know that oilskins aren't impossible to walk in—if you've next to nothing underneath. Then—yesterday—mist & fog & more mist so nothing doing outside but I darned socks & patched Thorgny's skirt (she's the one who teaches cookery here during the winter & is off to Finland for a year now. I've asked her to us next July! (Fru Blöndal says I can come here any time I like now!) You'd like Thorgný & she's a first-rate cook—hurrah so you'll get a rest from that next July—for one month at least. She's got neuralgia now poor soul—like Maisie's but is going to have electric treatment in Copenhagen on her way to Finland. Impossible here of course—no electric light. Then—who should turn up (I saw his rucksack first) but—Auden, the Oxford poet! He wrote "The Dog beneath the Skin" "Dance of Death" & other things besides poems. And he's producing a book on Iceland! (After two months or so &

not knowing the language but that's the way to do it—either at once or—at long last. It'll be amusing I expect and critical but I wonder if they'll like it. Though they're self critical & like it when foreigners slate 'em sometimes. Well—I made his bed for him & showed him in after we'd had a walk up into the mist together. He has a German emigrée wife, daughter of Thomas Mann the writer who's now exiled in Switzerland. I like him. He's taught English and is to do W.E.A. work at Manchester this coming winter but is meditating stopping at Egilsstöðum instead. I somehow don't think he will. He's roamed about a good bit—Portugal, Rumania, Greece. We played rummy till midnight he & Astrid & Fru Blöndal & I. This morning I continued patching—he's writing (borrowed paper from me) & Astrid is weaving. Windy but sun out & mist clearing away to-day, hurrah. There'll be more raking to-morrow I expect praps even to-day. I told Auden how I was doing Iceland. He's going round Langjökul with a group of four plus guides & tents in August—horseback.

Sunday. 11. 30. a.m.

And breakfast just over! Well it's a far cry from last Tuesday indeed. That same afternoon late-ish Auden & Astrid & I went over the "fljot" (find-river) to the doctor's house at Brekka. We had a grand dinner—grouse & patties and skýr—no, some kind of fruit porridge, because relations had come—about twenty-five at table. Then we just hung about waiting to hear if the doctor could see us. Auden had met a colleague of his in Seyðisfjorður. About 4. 15. we heard he could and set off, after cocoa & chocolate éclairs (at the house of some of the guests who were here to dinner). It was a glorious afternoon—hot, really hot, and sunny and it was deliciously cool to be rowed over the fljot—all milky-white-green. And the doctor was rather a dear with a pleasant plump fair-haired wife and two very nice small children one Ragnheiður, whose name I guessed aged three (two?) t'other a bit older. We had coffee & pancakes (about 7.) & jam (tradit[l] Icelandic cakes) & then Astrid & I went out with the good lady of the house & the kiddies, while Auden pumped the doctor about his practice—it's about twenty-five farms & all scattered miles from each other, he has the fljot in between, too & that takes at least 20 mins to cross, and a horse. Sts he's so busy he hasn't a minute to read, other times he's nothing to do for days. He reads chiefly English though some German too, but he didn't speak neither did his wife so Astrid & I were hard at it interpreting. They said they'd, or the doctor at least did, missed us while we were out! There were three rooms downstairs fitted out as a hospital ward & he'd a radium-lamp. Skin diseases disappeared within last 7 yrs; he performs operations sts in the farms if urgent; doesn't use chloroform 'cept in cases of childbirth (otherwise ether only) has a nurse to give the anaesthetic (like England no professional anæsthetists pure & simple here). Cancer slightly on increase (or is it that they know what it is now?). Curious—Iceland is being swept by an epidemic of measles at the moment—they're in the South, Akureyri and here—a boy of 15 in the next farm died last week from them, but he'd got T.B. and had always been ailing and weak. T.B. there's a lot of, but the drinking of milk helps against that. The children never got enough earlier on & all the smoked, salt & sour stuff they eat during the winter was bad. Now, at least, in the N. & E. almost every farm has its little garden with potatoes, rhubarb, lettuce, radishes, carrots, beetroots & small very sweet white turnips that are delicious. This place of course is unusually well-stocked—we have green stuff every day! Well, after further talk about 9. p.m.—we set off over the fljot again—the doctor's boy (about the house) taking us over. His cow shed was a model one—all turf & stone but lined with wood (roof) & spotlessly clean, fresh earth everywhere. The passage over was glorious—in the sunset the best I've had yet—the colour of the water was that queer northern shimmering you only get near the Arctic Circle, & the snow-mountains up & down the dale south & north blue. And all the sky flushed rose as we walked home through the birches—little stunted northerners with a strong scent in the sun. It's called "odorata" & it is! And Auden talked—about the possibilities of the cinema as a medium for poetry etc: all interesting. And supper late & so bed. The next day he was going. Astrid & I spent an hour of the morning up in the woods sun-bathing! And it was really hot & the scent of the thyme was blissful. And hot, hot, that afternoon. I went in the "rutebil" (bumping lorry-bus that goes between here & the fiords twice a week) with him & we talked hard. The scenery was grand, but if it hadn't been for the talk I think I'd have been sick! It's so bumpy—I've got a cut & bruise on my head yet from one specially bad lurch. I'm not looking forward to the drive north again—but if fine you see the country. The ideal way of getting about is horse-back but alack that is dying out 'cept for tourists which makes it expensive. And it takes long of course. One time it'd be fun to buy a horse & use it here & sell it again at the end of the time! Well I talked

Icelandic to the chauffeur who comes from Reyðarfiörður and who wants to come to England some time. His brother was on a boat for some time & speaks English & is teaching him now. Then I went out into the far fields & raked—not so fast and there was much laughing between the lads & lasses already there. Supper—tasted their blood-sausage steeped in sour milk for first time & found it much better than I'd thought it'd be. Thursday—hurrah—was as glorious & Fru Sigrún Blöndal planned an expedition—on horse-back to Hengjifoss. Off we set about 10. 30. am in brilliant sunshine with clouds piled up & Siggi the 11-year old boy (her son) who looks after hens & cows (he began doing that last summer) came too. It was rapturous. That's the only possible word. To ride all up yon rocks & down past the little waterfalls & over the streams and along the strand & through the bogs and up to Hrafnkel's farm (a Saga farmer) & so to the ferry. We had one halt about half-way when we let the horses loose & lay looking at the sky & the beginning of the far-distant waterfall across the "*fljót*". Then—the first thrill of the day—crossing in a horse-ferry! And the horses swimming behind us & us holding on to their reins. We went two & two because the stream was too strong to take all four animals at one & same time. It was just a shallow, low boat with water & hay at the bottom & the horses had to be kept from coming too near. One shivered—it's glacial water—even on a hot day & one was frightened but they're very good. Wish I'd had my camera—but as I can't take snaps it doesn't so much matter. I wish I could. And the second time—(Siggi & I waited by the "bagga" the man had brought over from t'other side of the river—great bundles of hay all trussed neatly) we took his dinner with us—his & t'others who were out there hay-making—a great blue can of coffee & food in a bowl of enormous dimensions tied up in a blue & white handkerchief, we'd had the grouse remains from Wednesday for breakfast—(grouse for breakfast!) so didn't feel hungry. (It's tinned or frozen of course as it's too early for the real bird). And so on & up over the mountain, slow progress picking our way over boulders & down over streams & through boggy patches. And so to a grass-grown patch high-up with an old *toft*-depression (grass-walled house) in a convenient spot & sheltered from the wind which was getting up. Dried fish & a smoked mutton & cheese sandwich (rye-bread) & then Siggi & Astrid & I descended & then began a scramble over great boulders & through rushing water up to the fall. It took an hour! Sts along slippery ledges sts wading knee-deep sts giving

Siggi a back—he hadn't high boots on. It was worth it too when we got there—it's the 2^d highest in Iceland & falls absolutely sheer for *c*. 360 feet! (at anyrate c. 120 metres) first just one slender sheet—slender because of height & then as it nears bottom it seems to branch underneath like candlesticks & the spray rises like smoke from the deep pool at the very bottom. We got quite up to it & the spray was like rain in the air. On way back I slipped across a specially tricky bit from a sloping wet ledge to a stone half under water & a long side-step but only got the water into one boot & had a wet knee which didn't matter a bit as the rain came on in a steady down-pour not long after we got back up to Fru Sigrún. It's rather fun riding in rain too & the dale spread out below looked like the pictures you get of river basins in atlases—only much vaster. And the wind was at our backs & the mist drove up over the hills opposite & shut out Snæfell who'd been glorious in the morning. So, about 6. 30. we came to Kloster farm where we had coffee & pancakes & jam & cream & waffles & *kleinur* (little twisted doughnut like things) & biscuits & cheese & sponge-cake! All most acceptable to wet-through folk—at least my nether part was—Astrid's cloak is more practicable than my sou-wester jacket if I haven't the trews as well & I didn't take 'em they were so heavy but I shall in future. I was afraid I'd make her sofa damp! Then about three hours later when we'd seen the house & I'd read a poem about a man buried in the churchyard of the monastery of which only grass-mounds remain, written by the great Canadian-Icelander poet Stéfan Stéfansson, we set out. Every Icelandic farm has a harmonium & oleograph & pictures like the ones you sts see in seaside boarding-houses belonging to mid-Victorian days. It's queer that the pictures are so bad when their taste in literature is so critical. There was a waterfall worked in silk, framed. I like the hand-woven upholstery of chairs & sofas & bedspreads best. And there are innumerable photographs always. But too, always books. I noticed that the parson (we visited his widow yesterday) of this district had several English books—Bertrand Russell, chiefly, but also Ogden's A.B.C. of Psychology (he's a Behaviourist) & Streeter on the Scolia, and a translation of Giovanni Papini's Life of Christ, and also of "Anne of Green Gables" (curious mixture). And Oliver Lodge (there's much spiritualism in a mild way here), besides Scandinavian books. And a desk, rocking chair, then other ordinary ones, cupboard, bookcase & photographs and harmonium (specially big one—it belonged to the church). Well, about 10. p.m. we set off, and this time—*rode the river*. That was fun. First we splashed through a long stretch of bog-land with white bog-cotton glimmering in the twilight that set in early after the wet afternoon. But no rain just mist & an unearthly stillness no wind & quiet as quiet. Then the river—all white and a strong current. And the man who knew where to cross took us two & two on each side of him & we waded—my horse was a bit frightened at first but it was better the 2^d & 3^d patch—it's very broad & we were a long time getting over to the other side. But they never had to swim actually—that's a bit difficult as sts they roll over & off you go! They were only up to their nostrils & the water only came up to our knees while sitting on horse-back! But it's a queer sensation—the green-white cloudy stream rushes past & neither horses nor you can see anything & there may be deep patches & quicksands & it's twilight & no sound but that of the animals pushing their way through & the desolate flood glimmering all the time. There were sand-patches & little beaches here & there—three strips of fiord or river or lake to cross. It's more like a great wide lake than anything else—the fljot. And then—gallop a gallop to get the horses dry & warm—great fun & Sproti, mine, was a fine feller & simply legged it after Siggi who had a real spirited beast. I can't imagine anything more satisfying than cantering thus along a lake-side or the hill—they're so sure-footed you don't bother about holes or stones or anything! And the twilight & the silence deepened and ahead, far ahead at the other end of the dale rose cold blue mountains streaked with snow & the water glimmered & glimmered. It was midnight (but like 9–10. p.m. at home now I s'pose & it *stays* like that no change for an hour or so). Then the steep toilsome ascent of rocks & stones & the crossing of streams & suddenly—the rush of scent from steaming birch-woods up to meet us as we climbed the crest that dips down to Hallormstaður. It just went to my head & I felt quite giddy for a few moments with it. Then it passed over & we got down into the little birch-wood itself—couldn't see the bluebells (harebells) shining amongst the clover in the grass at that hour!) At 1. 30. am. we reached home. Siggi & I took off the saddles & led the horses across the stream & out onto the moor. Then cheese & smoked mutton & rye-bread & milk & coffee in the kitchen. At 2. am—it was light! And almost broad daylight when Astrid and I had finished washing—we were that muddy after the rain. Friday—a quiet day. We stayed in all the time—mist hung about & it was inclined to rain—I read & darned socks & read part of Prometheus Unbound with Fru Sigrún—

she's interested in poetry. And we talked. And then—out a walk in the stillness of the evening. Queer light—mauve-primrose-buff over the distant mountains & wet freshness everywhere else. And that brings me to yesterday. Glorious, windy-fresh though little sun till midday for one brief moment. (I luxuriated in hearing on Wednesday that play at Wimbledon was postponed owing to rain & it was our first *really hot* summer's day here!). And all of us even Hr Blöndal set off and we picked up a man on the way who saw Fru Sigrún fall into the bog off her horse. It was exciting for one moment. The others had ridden on & were up over the rocky hill rising out of it. Suddenly, with no warning, her horse just in front of me, sank up to his shoulders, struggled in the brown slime, sideways, & flung her off— she was (fortunately perhaps) riding "saddle" i.e. "side-saddle" & fell where it wasn't so deep so all was well. The man, a pleasant fellow with a squint but astounding nice eyes & yellow wind-jacket took me round to a safe place. We'd attempted a too short, short-cut! And so up on the windy highlands—across moor-tracks—with blue snow hills far behind to the north & we riding towards great dark-blue peaks with snow thick in the hollows. On & on up the dale to a grass pasture—thyme & berries & thick rich grass & a burn gurgling deep below—we'd come round what was almost a precipice. And then on into a dead man's valley. Just gigantic sand-hills if you can imagine 'em thousands of feet high sloping down at 60° & 45° on each side to a wide valley of stones & sand & grit all sand, brown-buff, grey-brown & no sign of life & cotton-wool fog rolled up at the end over the river you could just glimpse under the thinner mist below. But sunshine when we stood at the north end—& green grass, brilliant & waterfalls frolicking down, and one particularly beautiful one, dropping sheer like Hengjifoss, only not quite so high only about 150 feet or so. And so back again—nine of us now. We'd stopped for coffee at a farm with a real old eld-hús (kitchen) of turf & stone—you went in through a long dark passage constructed thus & passed it with its hole in the roof & great mouldering bits of meat & sausage & fish hanging up & a huge copper over the hearth for boiling the mutton in, in September. Also the *bur* (larder) all turf & stone & earth with long wooden tub & pestle for making butter & tubs & boxes & vats. But the living-room was all wooden—just plain board walls & floor & nothing on 'em but photographs (only a few) & chairs, and the usual cupboard & sofa. On our way back we were there again (the man & wife came with us up the ("dead man's"

Letters from Iceland 1936

valley) for skýr & milk. And so on past the little church standing out grey with its scarlet tower against a deep blue-violet mountain with the snow rose-flushed in the sunset & towards the ever glimmering, primrose water. Coffee & pancakes it was about 9. p.m. then. And then—on & on & on along the lake-side in that same twilight. And over the moor by the lake with the great dark snow mountains looking only a few minutes ride away, to the left & pale ones through mist behind & Snaefell ahead & the water just to the right below. It's glorious to ride & ride & ride (even if you get a bit stiff on your seat whiles & your horse is lazy & needs much persuasion with a birch-switch!) I'm pleased I can ride with the others—it's the quick riding that tells of course & being on horse-back so many hours at a stretch! 10. 30 $^{a.m.}$–1. 30. *a.m.* & 11. 30–11. 30. with a day in between isn't so bad! Tho' of course we have many rests & are greatly refreshed by coffee etc: It's the jogging the Icelandic equivalent of a trot that's worst—because you can't rise as you do in England—they're not big enough! Now I've scribbled myself out & this is up-to-date—what a budget . . . What a screed! Oh—another amusing meal—last—no night before last— whole cods heads & liver! Most satisfactory and terribly good especially the liver! And filling to a degree!

            Bank Holiday. (Also here).
And two or three people have come with a couple o' tents—that's all. And this is as it were a show place "beauty spot" (what a word). Isleif, the almost two yr old's name for me is Aletta from "Hvað er þetta" which means "What's that"? So Hrafn is A.B.C. & I am "What's that"—good names both. Alack, today we depart—a fortnight and two days more & gone like smoke. It's been exceeding good here. Yesterday we just stayed in—I wrote of course—and Astrid read. Then an hour or so's gentle saunter à cheval up the mountain—it's over 1000 feet but everything looks so much smaller & nearer than it really is in the air here. I fell off first time on way home through the dwarf birch wood—branch caught first Sproti (horse) & then me—over the nose but he just waited. Sts it was like coming down a slag-heap. It's fun riding here—they're so surefooted.

{ Egilsstaðir. Monday.
August 3rd c. 8. P.M.

Yet another experience entirely new—a ride—about two & a half hours on a lorry (held coal last) *outside*—with the rucksacks & a tub of butter & sack of salt & bundle of rhubarb & saddle! Bumptity—bumptity—hop-là—down the hills & over the streams and up round the bends—once I was almost "thrown"—the bolt-hook I was clinging to with me right hand jerked out of place—it kept one of the "sides" of t'lorry in place! The sides were only a little over a foot high & I sat on a box back to lorry-driver & his two companions "inside" passengers, to wit, Astrid & an Icelandic girl. But the scenery was glorious—impressive in the still weather—mist over the mountains but cocoons of cloud too—swathed round 'em spiral-like & curious to behold & they deep blue. Wild, wild, & desolate & inspiring, & spacious and good to be alive in. I put on me oilskin trews before half-way—it got so cold exposed to a' the airts. "Inside" was so hot from engine I'd ha bin sick I'm sure. Then—here—invited to hot coffee by Astrid's friends & Kristlýn's the nice teacher in a beautiful wine-coloured Icelandic (what dye call that velvet that has deeper fluffier velvet on it?) dress. To-morrow for Ásbirgi—we stop once on the way to Akureyri praise be—I like not Icelandic "buses"! The Blöndals *were* nice. Now I must proceed with my Icelandic epistle to Hildur.

Thursday. Ásbyrgi.
The home-field
a little sunshine but very overcast.

Oh lordy lordy! How am I to convey something of it to you? First that night at Egilsstöðum. It was hot—& they had heating on or some such *and* our beds were literally broken down—at least Astrid's was—the straw was just like waves and a foot high in some places & a violent slope! *And* there was not only the usual featherbed on top—that is the only covering you ever have—but ditto, bigger & heavier underneath. Well I didn't actually sweat but it grew so hot—and only a tiny square of window that pushed open outwards two inches! I got up at 1. 30. a.m. & ransacked both beds—hurled the featherbed underneath into a corner of the room—only one available—t'was very small & only involved heaving it & then Astrid's over the end of my bed, lay down on the straw covered with sacking

& felt better. But at 6. the sun was so hot that not long after I lepped up & enquired me way to the tarn I knew existed over the hill. It took about twenty minutes walking & running to reach—in glorious fresh morning air & *hot* sun—over bog, through stunted birch undergrowth over little hills—Snaefell away over moor & mountain white & shining with snow & other dark blue hills striped like zebras. I plashed through bog to the tarn—gloriously deep at edge but reedy so I didn't swim just lowered myself in up to the ears & luxuriated & revelled in the cold brown water—second bath since I came here only! And better than the one Auden had I bet. I don't want warm water in a proper bathroom—out on the moor is so glorious—only sheep & wild birds & mountains & stillness—no wind. And after drying partly in sun but t'was cool by the tarn, I knelt down & washed me hair & that was refreshing. It was dry by the time I got back for breakfast at 8. 4.5. The bus came about 9. 30 & so we packed & off we sailed, at least it was sailing at first especially after the lorry-bumping the evening before. Away away & up over heath and with queer-shaped snow hills in the distance only two or three rising up like animals' heads from the flat. Then across Jökulsá a glorious river but water the colour of dirty washing water after muddy stockings—grey-black & froth like soap-scum. Very ugly but interesting & racing along a narrow gorge. Up & up & then a pleasant grassy tún with biggish f-house for dinner—fish & rhubarb-porridge. Then— across the desert. It *is* a desert. Nothing whatever but stones, stones, stones mile after mile. Then stone—sand mountains—greyish-black & brown—no colour—then black & black ash-grit everywhere— grey-black sand. And no-one spoke—down into valleys & always the same & up over stone-heaths. It's worse than a sand desert in the south I think because it's deader & further north & colder. No oasis—no sign of life & dead still only the bus bumped & jolted & jerked & rocked & swayed & bumped and yet we weren't going more than thirty miles at the most. On & on & on. Then a change up higher & a sprinkling of grávið the grey leaved shrub that grows everywhere here on the moors. And up over sand-grit mountains with only tiny buttons of thyme thrusting straight up from the stones to—the most impressive spectacle I've yet beheld. Imagine the land just dropping almost sheer away on all sides—narrow streaks of water cutting across the flat, and enormous Herðubreið (Broad Shoulder) blue & slightly snow-streaked rising up broad and massive—this shape →

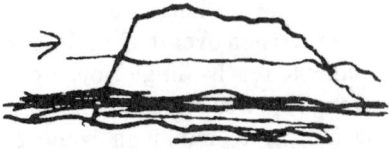
& beyond lone peak after peak. And still beyond—smooth like ice-cream brilliant white and the shape of a tiny segment of a gigantic circle —Vatna-jökul the biggest glacier in Iceland. And all blue—deep navy to pale sky—and the flat ground brown—mahogany to buff—no other colour from that height but the white strip in the far distance. And then from the flat—sinister dead black cones—in queer semi circular rows! extinct volcanoes. It was extraordinary. Beautiful, but at the same time these things were evil. Some mighty & absolutely ruthless & meaningless force had heaved & struggled and burst itself there. And then down into that flat and across—& down in it was bog-land &—one of the men has just come out & is mowing the short grass in great wide strong sweeps—it's heavy & wet from the rain last night & falls in thick rich heaps—he's quick. I'm sitting out in the homefield on some planks & poles piled up agin one of the heaps of dried dung that they use for fuel here—thin square tough cakes. And it is still 40° no sun now. Well—down in the flat bog—with brilliant yellow green grass & a sheet of bog-cotton—never have I seen such bog-cotton fluffy & glistening and dancing. And all browns & blues & no other colour in the distance. Then—a dreary dale stones & grey-shrub & no shape to the hills above. And then another worse stone-desert, mile after mile. Then sand-dunes but all black and wild corn waving on 'em everywhere. And the sand had come & eaten up the river it was choked as we splashed across it—there are of course few bridges & cars & buses just plough their way across rivers, sometimes well over two foot deep. And some of the sand clumps looked like giant hedge-hogs nose down and nose up chewing or sniffing. Then—more stones—utter desolation & a weariness to the spirit—what that place is like in bad weather I can scarcely imagine. And so by slow degrees to Grimsstaðir for coffee at 7. p.m. And then on & on—stones & heath & up & on & down & on & it grew twilight & a great heath of stones with here & there hideous clumps of lava like maimed & twisted hands & feet flung about. It was sinister & horrible. So down to Dettifoss roaring & raging & foaming & thundering its way down in an utter waste land. I'd not imagined it like that. And coming on it suddenly after a twenty minutes scramble down the stones & boulders of that waste

Páll

Halla

Jökulsdalur

Hlíðarendi

Transport

Árkvörn

Thórir

Thórsmörk

Letters from Iceland 1936

land from the stone-lava heath above was amazing. The water is the colour of water after muddy clothes have been washed—black-grey & the foam scum-like in the dimness. It was 10. 30 pm. when we were there. The fall is colossal & you're just stunned. It may have been partly that we'd had 13 hours of bus bumping before & through that terrifying scenery, but there is something frightful as well as beautiful about that fall. It's so gigantic & the scenery so absolutely naked & desolate that you forget even to be afraid—you simply marvel in a dazed, stupid fashion that such a thing can be! The water roared through the gorge—naked perpendicular columns of stone— & it's wide so that you can see the water twisting & turning for a bit. Then back up to the lava-heath & the stones & the last three hours of that bus were just a kind of nightmare—I should have said that you get hard blisters on your hands from gripping the rail in front of your seat—otherwise your head'd be cut open every few minutes from the bumps that send you up to the roof. And we swung & bumped & rocked—a bus does a terrific figure of eight then a bump & I understand how some folk are sick all the time. We had windows open so it was bearable. And at last down over another Jökulsá over a bridge & roaring mud-water rushing & swirling past below—& on over a black & grey beach of desolation to Lindabrekka—1. 30. a.m. We crawled out of that bus—bent double (you can only sit hunched up & crouched because of the vibration & the roof bumping! & slowly unbent & stretched & sorted out our luggage & decided what to do about the next day—we were 7 miles from place we wanted to be at but t'was too late to get off & enquire on the way & so—decided we'd have to get up at 6. next day to go in with a car that was picking folk up from this farm! That was a little grim & we sat down at 2. 15. a.m. to some thick stewed meat and blackest potatoes & sour bread & black blood-sausage rather silent. Then—as there were 15—we waited till they'd cleared away & put featherbeds on the two sofas in the eating-room for Astrid & me. It was, as you can imagine, hot—and broad daylight of course by then. At 3. we'd decided what to take with us in rucksacks here & crawled onto the sofas half-dead. And after 2½–3 hours sleep—up again! Coffee & cakes helped then more bumping & so here, 8. 30. a.m. more coffee & cakes & then we felt revived, walked to Ásbirgi itself. It's an amazing thing. You can judge of its size when told it takes fully an hour to walk up to the end of it & it's 360 feet high some places. It's a gigantic split in the earth nothing more or less & horse-shoe shaped

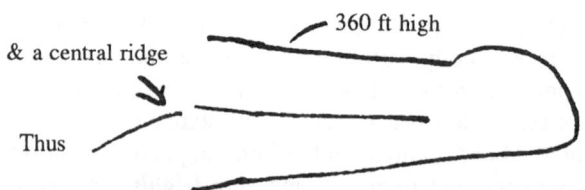

& it just rises from the flat—the sea isn't far off here—we saw the sun out over the black beach last night. To enter it is like walking into a place enclosed by this colossal horse-shoe shaped cliff—a cliff that runs for a two hours walk! and a central ridge. We walked round the edge the top—little dwarf birches & bilberries growing. Home to dinner at 11. 30–12. Then a nap. We've 2 rooms here! The bed we decided wasn't quite big eno' for us both just then & the 1st night here—Astrid's back which isn't ever very good was pretty bad after that bus-ride. I had one even! You feel you've been first bruised by being beaten all over & then cut in two. And—from the join in my ordinary knickers or the bus-seat? I had two huge red weals like whip-lashes on me end! I only noticed when I was washing & Astrid remarked! Well—I lay on some boxes covered with goat skins & sacking—rather narrow but I dozed. Up again at 2. p.m. & out a little. Coffee at 3. and then out into the great horse shoe. Heather—for first time in the moorland inside. Then—rain & it rained & rained—we splashed on to the end & saw the 60 feet deep pool or lake with the strange deep deep green water, & then through the shoe back—to the grey-black beach. Soaked—I had to change everything spite of me oilskin jacket—it's not fool-proof alack. Delicious to put on dry things & have a meal of rye-bread & flat rye unleavened cakes baked tough & flat as oatcakes on the naked stove, & eggs & cold cod & salt mutton & then hot porridge & sugar & milk. Last, after talk with the bóndi (farmer) coffee & cakes. And he spoke about the Sagas & Icelandic history & William Morris, whose daughter comes sometimes—she did 2 yrs ago. And we exchanged ideas about wine & tobacco & their uses he & I siding v. Astrid & so—to bed. I put on two coats & riding-breeks & me oilskin breeks & took the top cover from the bed & lay down on the boxes & goat-skins & sacking & slept the sleep of the just! It was even cold towards morning but I slept, now on one side now on t'other & now on back, now on tummy. And at 8. 15 went in beside Astrid so as not to let the nice woman of the house think that we weren't pleased with the bed. It is big eno' as a matter of fact & I think I'll sleep there tonight—

Letters from Iceland 1936

Astrid's back is better. And the sun came out a wee bit & coffee & cakes brought up to us in bed. There were even flowers—wee wild ones that grow here in a jar in the window & it *opened*! A tiny room just with bed & washing-stand one of those portable iron ones —& sloping wooden roof over the bed. It was delicious to cuddle down after! And blissful to sit out here. The sanitary arrangements are good—as so often—just the cow-shed but here it's goats! It's very simple, as it's all built of stones & turf, that grows roots dangling from the ceiling like sea-weed, & the floors & all are just hard-stamped earth. Doctors might advocate this Icelandic practice methinks as it's so auto-suggestive! That idea came to me as I mused there a few moments this morning—& it's spacious & roomy! You reach it via the hen-house, which is also the stable. All in order. You live much more in contact with the earth here—turf & stone just grow up out of it & one room leads to another & animals & human-beings are all animals together after all. Now this pole is hard so I intend a stroll. This is fun! To-morrow up at 7. again maybe 6 & bumped to Akureyri but in the meantime delicious here. Desolate heath to the north—mountains snow-striped west, stone table-land mountains east & moorland south—covered with tiny birch too. Now she's coming to say "Gerið svo vel" (dinner ready).

              Húsavik 11. 45. a.m.

En route for Akureyri—glorious weather just now—up since 7. a.m. about to have dinner. . . Address from *14th.*
    Poste Restante
      Reykjavik.
So long. J.

Goðafoss

V

Stafholtsey,
Borgarfirðum,
August 11. 1936.

And goodness only knows where the time goes! Rain—after three glorious days of sunshine—counting half-to-day as one. But I must go back to last week. Húsavík was where we stopped for lunch on the way from Ásbyrgi to Akureyri—a little fishing-village full of herring tubs & gleaming new casks in the sun, with snow hills across the water and queer lava wigwams decking the highway—one would make a perfect summer dwelling if the roof-hole were blocked or covered. It grew mistier later but was fair for Goðafoss which is a very graceful fall—I think actually more lovely though less sublime than Gullfoss or Dettifoss. It tumbles gaily—the others thunder straight down in uncompromising frightfulness. And the scenery was more blithe—rounded mountains not splintered peaks, and the colours soft and quiet. Then up & up & rain & fog but a rainbow too over a wild dale with a grey river winding & rushing. A gale of wind & then down towards Akureyri—the Eyjafiord stretching away out to sea to the right & the long dale to left—& Akureyri down on the opposite shore. We made good time—got there at 5. P.M. and were given coffee by the mother of Thorhild Astrid's friend with whom we stayed last—her husband teaches gymnastics in the big school there. Then—it rained! But we had a pleasant evening—two girls were also guests there (we had Thorhild's room this time) & one sang well, so does Thorhild's sister Inga who wants to come to England. It really was joyous. And ten or eleven of us there! just the family & us. Next m^g lateish up and then shopping & visit to Bank & so off at 1. P.M. up through mist but improving weather on to glorious high mts. It should have been the most exciting scenery yet but alack the rain came on this time in torrents so we saw nowt, after Svartardalur & the strip of glacier at the head of the dale. Then just rain & a long dale—well-named Langadalur! And a halt, most welcome, for coffee & slice after slice of rye & wheat bread & cheese & small cakes. That was late about 6. We just made our evening meal & when we reached Blönduós & the weather cleared hopped out for a walk by the sea instead of having dinner. The sheep were fine looking kritters & browsing hard on sea-weed—standing fearlessly up to their knees in sea-water & the tide coming in. I watched some eider-duck too. No-one there by the little pier—Astrid had packing to do so I just stayed out a bit. Then—up (Next day 10. a.m.) At that moment full stop because Pálfrey came to say that she was ready to set out to Langholt her brother-in-law's farm so off we went through rain & all—& I had the best horse I've yet had & he just *went*—"valgallop" over the moor tufts & all! And the brother-in-law & his wife, being great sportsmen were out salmon-fishing in Hvítá the best river in Iceland possibly. So over another stretch of wet moor the rain increasing, down to milky Hvítá (White River—so-called because the glacial water is quite white). And didn't the woman Jórunn land a trout of fair size just after we arrived & then—he a nice little 16 lb salmon—and then—all within half-an hour—she an 18 lber! It was thrilling to watch. Paddywag & Scott would have rejoiced. But imagine—three fish & of such dimensions in half-an hour! And Björn got a 20 lber an hour or two later—she came back home with us & gave us glorious hot thick cream & cakes & we talked. An Englishman called Wenner (a "captain") (M.B.O.V. whatever that may mean) goes there every summer—he has a big place in Shropshire sg Hall. After—back to Björn with more worms & some grub for himself too & we galloped home with the salmon she took in a sack. And it was dark—11. 30. before we got back (by their clock. It's a bit confusing whiles here. There's no Summer Time but each farm does that which is right in its owner's eyes as regards time in the summer. So that, the wireless clock, as they call it may be two hours or more behind theirs. Thus on our way here we had dinner at 12. 30. & then coffee (equivalent of tea) at 2. p.m. (it was 4. p.m. by the clock on that particular farm!) To revert to Saturday—no Sunday morning, start at 7. and perfect weather—hot sun & glorious colour—past old turf & stone farms & fields of bog-cotton fairly blowing in the wind.

Friday 13th. 11. 30. am.

Brrr–r–r. Snow now—covering the hills Hafnarfjöll near by & a blizzard of rain & wind. And we were out riding till midnight again yesterday afternoon! It was cold—horses couldn't go fast because of mud—about 2 foot of it some places. But it was fun. But to revert to the journey on Sunday last. At about 12. 30 we reached a place by a lake with a queer extinct volcano & little birch shrubs & glorious view—Baula over 3000 feet rising in a perfect round fat cone thus ⋀ above t'other mts. And fed there. Then on to Hvítárvellir in glorious sun—blazing and fresh breeze. And Eiriksjökul (glacier) rose semi circularly blue and snow capped and then Langjökul and then yet another all shining white in the distance. And Hafnarfjöll jagged & peaked & dark blue running out to sea. And to the west (they are S.W. from here yet more mountains curving mostly. And a huge plain of brilliant bog—green, green with tarns & pools & reeds & bog-cotton all shining in the sun. And we waited four hours or so happily at Hvítarvellir for Páll to come from here—Stefanesey (in middle of the bog) with the horses. And the folk here were charming, gave us coffee & then fruit salad (tinned of course—tho' they do grow red currants there) and before we set off milk! And then we drank coffee on the way & had supper when we arrived! As it were four meals within six to seven hours. Well, the first morning Monday was blissful—hot, hot & we made hay with vigour & continued late so as to have it all safe in because Páll was afraid it'd rain. It was blissful—smell of hay and glaciers far off under a blue clear sky and all the hidden colour shifting with the time o' day. The two girls who're here for the hay-season are nice—one with red-gold hair, blue dungarees over a white blouse with short sleeves and brilliant light purple woolly gloves. T'other dark in a brown short-sleeved blouse, blue bib & brace. And both so sun-tanned. And the man is the son of a doctor in Reykjavik—he's only 18 or so I should say & it's his first summer out "in the country". Students often take jobs like this in the summer. When it's weather like to-day it's hard—Páll & the boy Snæbjorn Jónsson were out mowing in that blizzard and all! But the girls were in. Well—Monday just melted away under sun. Tuesday morning was good too but not cloudless and I raked for first time in bog, barefoot & with heavy reed-grass—it was fun—refreshing & cool & the brown water squelched, squelched—it's up to one's knees almost! Then after dinner—they've many here—Páll the farmer & his wife Pálfrey, then her mother, and a delightful woman of 70! red-cheeked dark-haired & looking about 45 she works like a man & has been here summer after summer—has pains in feet & legs often but only wants to be able to go on working thus—Guðlaugr. Then their children—two boys & a girl, the boy's just out of bed after measles (there are measles all over the island—every farm's had one case or another). Then a girl who helps in kitchen & another who is out with the kiddies but who makes hay sts too. Then the hired folk—the lad from Reykjavik & the two girls. So Astrid & I are treated like guests & have meals in the parlour. After dinner Tuesday Pálfrey & Astrid & I rode over to Langholt the neighbouring farm across a bog, a river & over a little hill—where Páll's brother lives. But I've told you about that afternoon. We heard last night when we called in from our way from Reykholt that they caught 6 salmon in all Tuesday & 8 yesterday & one was 22 lbs! We had salmon-trout & new potatoes & skýr for dinner yesterday. Then out to Reykholt on horse-back. (I mowed or tried to a little between 11. 30 & 1. We get up almost 10 here!) That's where Snorri Sturlason, the greatest medieval historian, lived. There's a High School there now (Danish H.S. type) where boys & girls from 16 up (no age limit) spend the winter & read Icelandic literature & history & Danish, a little English and learn some hand-work. It's all heated by steam from the hot springs. This dale is called Reykjadalur because it's full of springs—the steam blows up all the time—it's funny to cross a swirling deep cold glacier river and yet pass by a spring gushing up from the bottom! And the water in some of the streams is quite hot. We had coffee at a farm which was so heated & saw the big boiler in the kitchen. You can't bake with the steam so they usually have stoves as well. Snorri's bath is outside in the garden (there is a garden there) and the water's too hot to get into—circular & about 10 feet across. The colours on the way there were glorious—deep, deep blues & purples & brilliant greens on the homefields & pale blue glacier mountains. *Then* came the rain—swirling & soaking. We just got to the school in time to be mildly wet—(it takes time to unsaddle the horses & let em out to pasture & fix up the wire fence after). Hot coffee & cakes again & talk & we saw over the school. They sleep bunk-wise 6 in a room. Then a cold ride home—snow falling on the hills. A halt at Langholt—Astrid's horse bolted before we got there—over a huge stretch of grey stone-and-sand (the work of the river Hvítá). It was a grand sight tho' a bit alarming at first—I don't know how Astrid sat on but she did—he startled my beastie so that he swerved violently but didn't follow he was too good "þýður". But she flew off like an arrow from the bow & they must have galloped a mile or two before he stopped—her black cloak streamed in the wind & that frightened him & the faster he went the more it flapped. We went after and then she turned. So she wasn't cold—when we got to Langholt. There, they gave us milk & cakes & Björn "the hunter" showed me his boxes of salmon-flies—beauties—I only remember the names Golden Eagle, Dusty Miller, Shock Scot, Yellow Grub, but he had dozens & one "Dr Blöndal" (after his brother who died) which he thinks best. He's caught salmon weighing nearly 40 lbs in Hvítá! Daddy & Scott'd have been thrilled that Tuesday—I was—& then yesterday passing by didn't we see him land a 22 lber! Of course it's not always as good as this—this wild wet weather after a spell of sun & heat is good but I call a catch of 14 salmon in a day & a half pretty good going don't you? And such beauties, fat, fat & their skin pearly-blue-green-rose & silver. Well—after milk etc: once more up—(I'm never stiff now hooray spite of riding on soaking saddles & getting wet on the knees—but I wore me oilskins yesterday a–ha!) & a slow j^y through dark bog in wind & rain. And it was good to tumble into bed under a featherbed & all—I have the sofa here—it's a nice wide one. Astrid the bed as I *can't* sleep *between* featherbeds. "Enough is as good"—Well—that's up-to-date. To-morrow to Reykjavik. Then Saturday afternoon out to Fljotshlíð in the south to another Páll at Ákvörn. I must send this from R. & ask about post. Now *N.B.* could you send to *Poste Restante, Reykjavik*.

(1) *A recipe for mint jelly*. The nice folk at Hvítárvellir had their garden a blowing with mint, mint almost three feet high aromatic & green, & they didn't know what it was nor how you could use it! So I told 'em & promised 'em a recipe for mint jelly (they can use it in the winter then). Hasn't Mrs Morley one? If you haven't?
(2) *One £1 note*. I forgot to save 2 for my return ticket from Hull & have only £1 in English currency & an English £1 note is not to be had here for love or money. They can't obtain any foreign currency.
. . . It's been snowing here! Brr–r—autumn's come a bit early.

14th Reykjavík.

Well—well got your budgets all three at last only to-day the middle of August and it was good to get 'em. And I've answered the one wot needed dealing with. Well since yesterday what? Up at 5. 30. am. and after a meal of hard boiled-eggs, cheese, *cold pancakes* & *cocoa*! gallop-a-pace over bog & moor & through river & stream & puddle the mud just feet deep after the rain—to catch a milk-lorry to take us to Borgarnes to catch the boat for Reykjavík! Well—one river was too much for us—we'd have been soaked to middles & more & as we had a j^y before us we decided to turn back in mid-stream & dashed along the banks to find a ford. That was glorious just splashing along towards hills blue-green under mist-clouds with new fallen snow on 'em, & rainbows gleaming about and the strong smell of rank wet hay smoking in barns. And we saw the milk coming 2 cans tied on to each horse pannier-wise & that was duly dumped with us

at the roadside. And along bumped the lorry already half-filled with great cans & a bicycle & a lorry-tyre & fishing-rods & sacks and parcels & one wee man. We were 8 by the time we reached Borgarnes, & I was *lying* on some cans in front & rejoicing in me oilskins wot kept aht the wind. It was like January! But the sun came out at Borgarnes at 10. am. & the voyage though roughish was only 3 hrs— I slept part of it. And now, correspondence, seeing people, going out to meals & washing—then to Fljótshlíð in the south to-morrow afternoon. It is such fun. But alack good-bye to Astríd on Monday there—she sails for Sweden Tuesday—term begins early. She was here all June almost—She sends much love, I do too to everyone.
                                                                                                Jean.
Do hope Madge & Maisie & R enjoy their holiday & that you did. Love to Stella when she comes please. Astrid sends hers too.

Páll

Halla and Thórir

Lunch in the meadow

VI

Árkvörn.
Fljótshlíð.
10. 30. A.M. August 17. 1936.

This—is the real thing—Astrid graded it well—and now thoroughly acclimatised, food-ised—attitudinised as it were I enter on a stimulating phase of experience as a fully-fledged "matvinningur" (literally—"food-winner"). And I think I've passed *the* test [*N.B. Censor here* for male readers if this epistle happens to be read aloud—they being the more susceptible sex (but all the same I don't mind two sensible specimens like the Paddywag & Wagskall perusing this in private!) The test I take it is to walk quite openly first, through the room the door of this opens into—a wee narrow slit of a room between doors, but boasting of a window which the two lads who sleep there don't open, through the kitchen, through the passage at right angles to that leading past two guest-rooms—or "parlours" out at the porch, down two steps, along past various cow-houses, to the erection very narrow & door all swinging in the wind & has to be tied up with string every time you enter & one hinge the bottom one missing, and so to the dung-heap adjacent (Icelanders *do* believe in Suggestion!) and sling there the contents of the *pot-de-chambre*! And you may meet any or all the inmates of this farm en route, within, or without. Astrid met Páll the farmer himself her first morning here in June. The window only opens two inches outwards a sloping casement like the top one in my room at home so it's not possible to water the plants in the garden (Astrid says it's good for them!) Well, this morning I was fortunate only one lad lying on a sofa reading—of course they think nowt of it so that's O.K. Then here I'm on proper Icelandic country rations—damp rye-bread & butter (it's terribly good I think, flat hard baked rye-"oatcake", bits of salt-smoked beef—very strong & good to chew and—

11. 30. P.M.

At that moment (10. 40. am.) Halla, Páll's wife sent Gísli one of the men-workers here, a lad, to say I was to go out to "the meadows". They were half-an-hour from the farm right up the mountain—all precipitous & thrilling—you heard the scythes being sharpened over your head as it were. Well Gísli and I raked in silence about two hours or so—only the sound of the river rushing over the huge expanse of black grit below. He knew I was a "furriner". Then came coffee—rather cold after being taken so far in a can but still a break with sugar—we just lay on the wet grass & talked, Páll & Thori and Hreiðar and Gísli & I—I was the only woman. That would be about 1. P.M. Then we raked again till 2. 15 or so—but the rain which had been falling all the time before came on real heavy & we were soaked & then my rake bust (it was a bad 'un anyway) so off we went home G. & I. The others had been out since 7. & had their breakfast out. At home there was first changing—I was wet every stitch—then a heap to wash up while Halla baked. About 3. 30. a meal of very salt salt-fish-chunks, potatoes &—hurrah lettuce, followed by the inevitable cold porridge & some milk mixture. Then more washing-up of very fishy fishy utensils etc: Then ironing—a pile o' shirts, boys' coarse linen bibs & braces etc etc: etc: "rough-iron" Halla said & rough-iron it was. But life ain't monotonous. No—scarcely embarked on 5th shirt when Halla called would I chase the cows from the home-field where they'd strayed by mistake. Now thinks I, I'll keep me boots on this time—you never know when you'll be out in the mud. Half-a mile's chase enlivened by the antics of the dog Spori who had an animus for, violently reciprocated by, a particular angry-eyed cow. More ironing & meditations on life in general & on that on an Icelandic farm in particular. Halla calls— would Jóhanna (that's my name here & I'm "thou"-ed by 'em all & "thou" them which I like) go & find Bói (the 8-year old) who was "out somewhere" to tell him to take coffee to the mowers & rakers. It wasn't raining so much. Chase & shouting after Bói—tracked to farm on other side the stream & found in a hay-loft near a waterfall which accounted for his peculiar dulness of hearing! Incidentally, en route for Bói I plunged inadvertently into *their* dung morass which necessitated a second change of stockings at least (now only 1 pair left!). Resumed ironing—by this time 6. 30 P.M. (Up at 7. & saw Astrid off—walked 2½ miles there & back & back to breakfast at 9. 50. am.) Halla calls the cows are in the homefield again. This time one of 'em busy eating hay from a new-made cock. Wild dash over the homefield followed by Spori who again makes dead set at speckled cow with angry red eyes (no wonder), and a wilder chase down the bank to the river-bed shore all black grit and sand & stone & water (miles of it stretching away in front and the glacier rising to the left very near). Return after ¼ hour or so to farm—Resume & this time complete ironing. By now 8. 30 P.M. Halla still baking—

suggests first I might spread the bread for the evening meal which consists of spread bread (a kind of sweet dripping = goat's cheese really I find) on rye "oatcakes" & chunks of salt meat on damp "potbrauð" (rye-bread) & cold porridge & sour milk. Changes her mind & asks me to bake the rye oatcakes instead. This very thrilling—they're spread out on the bare stove pricked hard, turned, brushed over with water, piled up—about 18" across so thrilling to "turn". 9. 30. the men return washing of socks, changing of trews etc:—11 of us in the kitchen I sit turning oatcakes—they eat & talk. (I had "coffee" & some of Halla's "bake" at about 6. P.M.). Halla says will I go out & help Anna (the other woman-worker here) with the milk-cans—she milks. I'm going to learn if possible. We take big can down to stream & deposit it just under the waterfall to keep cool & fresh & standing knee-deep wash out wooden buckets etc: All the while cold—like winter at home & much mud etc: everywhere—also water & dark. Return to baking. At *10. 30. P.M.* quite finished & sit down to evening meal—spread bread but for me an egg as well & lettuce. Then—washing-up—finished everything at last by *11. 30.* And now Halla says I needn't be up by 7. like the others but lie as long as I like & I think I will! Well, well, well verra verra interesting. I wish you could have seen the kitchen—with the men swallowing their huge filled plates of sour milk & cold porridge, four of 'em & one who just called in attendant taking snuff (they all do in Iceland often)—Halla busy spreading bread, Anna washing her 4-year old boy in a corner by the cellar-door, two other lads somewhere else & me sitting by the stove turning cakes & exchanging remarks with the men. It's another existence altogether this, & yet, this is the queer thing about it, not strange, as if it had been before. Rain still descending alack—if it's bad I'm not allowed out & I'd rather be out on the mountain side really, even in rain than in the kitchen tho' the kitchen is interesting. Even washing up is exciting because you have to keep an eye on Thorir—the poor little 5-year old son, the only child of Páll & Halla—He's a complete idiot & has the mischievousness that they sometimes have—& at meal-times he just throws all his food about—milk & all, which makes things difficult sometimes. Astrid told me about him before I came. I didn't know before. It's grim for his parents. I can't help wondering what they'll do later on. Páll is charming—like Mr Geoffrey Phillpotts of Dublin only with blue eyes, a husky voice & he picks his teeth with his fork. It's odd how little things like that matter when the people themselves are so thoroughly good & thoughtful. For instance he brought me the 2^d volume of a book I'd begun reading at Hallormsstaðir before he went to bed & said to-day I was to go home & read & not rake any more. And Thorir just heard that I wanted the brush for the rye-cakes & handed it to me—that kind of courtesy what we'd call good manners is rare on the whole in Iceland, but underneath the primitiveness they're such fine folk. Halla is pretty—rather like Maisie & hardworking & cheerful—I like her. She told me to-day how relieved she was to find I was as I was! i.e. I could really eat their food and wash up & do odd jobs and not be bored. She asked me to-night if I'd been bored. Help! No too busy I might have replied—I honestly said no it had all been so interesting & it was such fun to see how everything was done on an Icelandic farm. She's short of a woman to help in the kitchen at the moment so is especially glad to have me. Now—12. 20 am. to bed, to bed, to bed. Thórsmark a dale all glacier & mountain surrounded is exceedingly beautiful even when descried only through rain & mist—this evening it went deep blue. Goodnight.

Tuesday Morning 11. a.m.

And I'm to be "free" for ½ hour says Halla so I snatched me pad & pen as these odd moments are literally the only ones I have to gossip to you about it all. Well—I did sleep and sleep this morning, till 8. 45 at least & since—have made me bed "done" me room i.e. the washstand with Astrid's discarded stockings—there's allus only one "clout" in Icelandic farms & I prefer Astrid's stockings just as they are! This pen wobbles as me hands ain't used to being first a long time in cold water then in boiling—also raking makes 'em stiff at first. Well—then I took several pairs of heavy socks down to the stream to wash under the waterfall medieval fashion on a flat stone with a wooden clapper (like the ones you see in Norwegian museums). That was rare fun—the sun tried to come out—& did for a bit. But—Thorir the 5-year old came too & it wasn't till both boots & socks had floated far that I realised he was taking off his clothes & flinging 'em into the water! Lord, lord, how does Halla manage at all. There's aye milk on the kitchen floor that he's spilt & the two dogs don't allus lap it all up, & butter on door handles & so forth. I think she's a marvel. Well after banging & rinsing & wringing the socks home to breakfast—of cold porridge & sour milk & rye bread & smoked sausage-fat, very good—also milk to drink. I've put on at least a stone alack—but must try to restrict my ravenousness here—but I'm terribly fit & well, what you might call "blooming" (that word allus suggests rotundity to me as well as red cheeks!). Then the chicks fed—with scrapings from the porridge-pot (that's the worst thing to wash up—it's just all stuck, & takes a good while to scrape clean. Then Halla said I might be free—ten minutes read now of a book I understand from within as well as from outside you might say— "*Independent People*" by Laxnes author of "Salka Valka"—which, if you read, take with much salt. No Icelander I've met is in the least like S. the man there—& many are like Salka Valka the heroine. Another mild "test" to-day was to eat breakfast next to the nice Gísli who'd just cleaned out the "*fjós*" (stable) Hooray, I've discovered my top-window does open just far enough if one stands on the bed & leans far out. Great comfort & joy to one who like Swedish Astrid still has certain inhibitions (They've quite gone after a week here!). Now for a read. Then I take coffee to the field-workers, who're still further off to-day & rake up the mountain-side hooray. It's so good to be out in that air with just the sound of the river rushing away down far below & the glacier glistening opposite & then that huge stretch of black sand & water fading into sea—westwards. This farm is just at the foot of a hill almost as high as Beachy Head, you see the sheep wandering about from the kitchen window & hear the waterfall. The name Fljótshlíð means Fljot- (water) side (Hlíð) and there are waterfalls every few yards almost some big. All the farms snuggle close under & have that gorgeous view.

9. P.M. Tuesday.

Back a wee while since from "the meadows" this time literally all along precipices & waterfalls spouting by & in bog-patches. It was so hot (!) at first only that I pulled off boots & stockings & was barefoot lovely when we came to patches of bog. Later it rained "showers" (*Icelandic* showers). I was soaked from slipping on some very steep places but dried later. Dinner at 3. 30 P.M. or 4. was divine great hunks of salt fish, potatoes swedes all from a tin pail—I had Hreiðar's plate (just "wiped" he was away getting turf to-day. Followed by rice pudding also good. We sat on the wet grass & talked— How alert & interested little Páll is—I watched him while I was resting a moment before coming home this evening—against Thórsmork which was beautiful to-day—giant mountains—tableland like say all blue dark & green & rose in sunshine & snow on the glacier opposite—We were I dunno how many feet up & whiles the slope was almost perpendicular—Icelanders have heads & feet like cats for slippery heights I find. And Páll little, slight but tough & strong was moving steadily & with quiet relish—agin that colossal background. And from time to time he shot questions at me—about ancient Irish literature—I'll have told him all I know soon goodness the insatiability of him—& tried to discuss religion & racial intermarriage—all rather difficult as he doesn't read English at all. Then more raking & just as it grew rather heavy—it is hard work raking lashings of soaking wet long bog-grass down & *up* perpendicular slopes!—came Bói the 8-year old with coffee & cakes—ah! And then the sun came out again—6. 15. P.M. c. It *is* good. Now there'll only be washing up at 10. P.M. this evening I think. What a good day. And I do like Anna the other woman who's here raking—Gisli is her son & there's a 4 year old Sigurður here too. She's a dear. Says it's such fun to be here away from her home & responsibilities—in Reykjavik & just raking—she milks cows too—otherwise we share the odd jobs between us. What strikes a body so forcibly about these people is that they enjoy their work so—it's all such fun—especially in the summer.

Wednesday. 11. P.M.

Just finished—right hand *stiff* from raking. Dry weather came blazing sun & north-east wind, the perfect combination & glorious to work in—it'd have been cold to sit out but in the homefield—heavenly. We were there to-day spreading out the stuff from cocks—then turning it in ‖ rows the way they do it here—then hauling it together, "saxing" it (dunno English equivalent as we don't do it)—& binding it in "baggar" (big roundish-squarish bundles to put pannier-wise on horse-back or on a little low cart. Next-door they were sledging it to the barn! And—before going out—I first washed meself in the pool under the second waterfall—brrrr—but good & awakening. Then a vest & breeks—then banged the men's socks per usual. Then breakfast at 10. Then washed up—lots & lots—& the things from the early breakfast they'd had out up the hills too. Then they all trooped back & out we flocked. Lord—it was beautiful—Astrid said it could be here. The mountains & glacier were a joy & the way waterfalls seemed to sing the way they streamed foaming down after the rain. And birds came from the sea & circled overhead calling—black & white with long red bills—and wee Thori (the 5-year old who's not there at all) enjoyed himself so, that one almost imagined he was normal. He has fair, fair hair & the bluest of blue eyes. And of course later—he sent a rake flying down the west-stream (the farm land is bounded by two deep wide streams fed by big falls lepping straight down the mountainside which is almost perpendicular above—& likewise both his boots which sank & were only spotted with difficulty. At 8. 30. P.M. it was time for him to come home so I carried him—the homefield is about 10 mins away from the farm—(where we fetched up yesterday on the mountain was a good hard 45 mins walk!!) And I felt rather a beast for being somewhat repelled at first—it was at the table it was difficilé—when he wanted to spit his food all over the place! It's queer that doctors can't do aught about that yet—it's probably only a cord nerve-end somewhere that isn't joined right. He tried to help out in the field—dragging the hay with us. And Anne's 4-year old was there too & Bói the funny little 8–9 year old who's been fostered here—one of a large family. He comes to watch me banging the socks & gives me advice—likewise when I bake the rye cakes. And he told me an old woman who became so ill she had to go to hospital & there she died of her illness—knitted his socks which I'd admired. She was Thorunn, Páll's mother. Astrid thought more of her than of any other Icelander she's met. She must have been a fine woman. Well—all day out in sun & wind rake—rake—raking & thinking & saying all of us at least once—what fun to be alive. It's so utterly incredible that in Spain things should be as they are. I hear fragments from the wireless & Páll comments on what is happening but I don't know at all and can't always understand his comments. They talk very fast & take it for granted I do understand as much as Astrid did! The river & waterfalls—we are walking under two big ones to-day, were like the sea. When I came in—(up at 8. 30) at 8. 30. P.M. I baked rye-cakes till 10:30 eating bread & porridge & milk while turning 'em & so to bed. Páll & the others came in while I was at it—& then we washed up. The men are still out some of 'em & it 11. 30 PM! And dark but for clear stars. What a glorious day!

Thursday. 20th.

Well my hand isn't too stiff to wield the pen—tho' it almost was after this 13 hour day. But I did have an hour off at 3. P.M. up the mountain-side when I snatched a sun-bath & lazed in the hay looking at the glacier. Lord—how good it is when the sun blazes as it did this morning. I'm completely burned & again went barefoot this time because it was so hot! Anyway it's the only thing to do (whatever the soles feel like when you get back) because you're always in bog or on the edge of precipices or sliding down right-angle slopes of several hundred yards long. How the men mow on these I dunno. Well first I again washed socks & trousers (that seems to begin the day always) no time for self (it involves going up stream a little) because I read in bed half-an hour instead. Then—we raked like mad in the homefield so that all was in by 12. 30. Then off up the mountain-side & at it till almost 10. P.M! And the fish & turnips were even better than last time, & we had pancakes with coffee. And when I got back Halla had done me a delectable chop (pork (back) with new potatoes & there was lettuce—the first English food I've had. But I felt ashamed to be eating that when the others, who'd been out since 6 am (! a 16 hour day) were just having porridge & rye-bread & butter. But it was because I'd worked all day—Páll said several times wouldn't I go home but I wanted to be in at the death—and had my reward—the most gorgeous really gorgeous sunset reflected on the glacier & the mountains up the dale that I've ever seen here—rose & purple, blue & the grey-black sand below with all the silver winding waters & the colour of the mts reflected in 'em. There was great satisfaction in being up there this day. Not that there's much time to look at the surrounding loveliness but you just know & feel & hear it's there. And during the hour "off" I almost *heard* the clouds that from time to time crept over the sun—it was so quiet. Gosh how I love Iceland. Good-night.

Saturday 22^d.

1. a.m. Sunday morning & I've just finished the day's work! Began by raining hard—so just baked & washed up. The telephone from farm which has phone 2½ miles off—boy brought the message. Donned oilskins & set off full pelt through *terrific* wind & rain (west wind though) to find out. T'was from Prof. Basset of Reading who's here too—coming s-east at end of next week. What fun! Then more washing-up, swept various floors, washed windows, mopped up pools on ledges (basin on one of the beds to catch the drips as in Ireland). Then the 8-year old who takes coffee to the men mowing on the mountain failed to make his appearance so I donned riding-breeks & set off with coffee & cakes in rooky about 6. P.M. Wild weather—but a broken arch of rainbow over the dale and the white tablelands & dark peaks beyond were worth going out for. Tremendous wind up

the mountain & the horse-path all slippery-mud—found the mowers after a good hour's ascent—they lay down on the soaking grass in pouring rain with oilskin coats over 'em like blankets & drank and ate—losh—do they never have rheumatics? (apparently it's *not* as prevalent here as at home all the same!). The rain lashed down in earnest—no rainbow or sight of blue on the way back. Changed & set to to iron. Porridge at 10. P.M. Then washing-up—then guests came four—more odds & ends & just finished last washing-up—Páll talking the while of Strindberg, Dante & Shakespeare—on the wooden bench by the sink. What a man & he up since 6. am. & mowing like mad in what we'd call weather not fit to send a dog out in—eating his fish out of the pail & all & drinking coffee as hot as might be expected after an hour's walk up a mountain in an enamel can! Well, well. And yesterday—hot again at first—what a long way off it seems. We finished up the mountain-cut hay—binding it—between about 10. am. & 7. p.m. Then home—helped Anna with clothes-hanging out (had rinsed some with her before going up the hill—in the stream—what a washing—of folk & everything including sheets & pillow-slips. Then—because we'd taken in all the hay from the homefield—we had *töðugjöld* (a feast of hot cocoa & pancakes & jam (it costs 1/2 a lb here) & cakes & coffee—all at midnight—in the sitting-room not the kitchen & we changed slightly—Páll put on his socks & a coat & I me one other dress. We'd all been in the homefield first thing & got that done in no time—t'was fun. Apparently you allus have this feast when all's in thus. So to bed after 1. am. & read till 2. am. as no time during the day. It clouded over up the mountains but was better to work in. Feet bled a bit from thistles & short cut grass so decided to indulge in pair of sand-shoes (they cost 4/- here!) So when I got back from the hills nipped on to Haki & cantered off to farm with telephone & where the Reykjavik rutebil stops. Haki was like the wind—what a glorious horse to ride—& I didn't fall off—Páll was aferd I would! The saddle lopped all off to one side but I didn't even so—it was too loosely fastened. Saddles often do that here & it's a bit awkward sometimes if it happens in the middle of a bog or halfway up a bank. And the dale mountains & glacier were aglow in the sunset as I came back. And they "thou'd" me in the kitchen at Mulakoti when they heard I'd been raking & helping in the kitchen here. Now—sleep—. 1. 30. Sunday morning early. Got yr letter to-day at Mulakoti—nice.

Monday. 11. 30 P.M.

Just got to bed—began at 8. 30. this morning. Baked for hour and half or so—washed socks (it pelted with rain so I rinsed em down in the "cellar" alongside the salt fish & smoked meats & bones & chicken food & general litter—& banged 'em in the stream clad in oilskin coat. Then fed & washed-up—a lot this morning as there's a "guest" here. Then ironed for hours. Then 1/2 hour off during which I read some modern Icelandic. Dinner at 3. 15. P.M.—usual salt fish & rice—then washed—(no I didn't for once as there was so much cut I lepped off to rake—raked like mad with ten minutes interval for coffee at 6. 45. P.M.—till 9. 30. P.M! And wet, heavy grass all up & down slithery slopes in rubber boots & trews & coat. Then home, supper of rye-bread & porridge—washed up—and then a grand wash—bath in my tiny basin (thorough, so it took no end of a time twenty minutes I think), and so to bed. Oh—I am sleepy—& on the way home—Páll asking all kinds of things about words—& me panting to keep up down the mounting, let alone finding phrases to answer him in Icelandic! Well—I may never write a book on the ancient Icelandic woman but I do know a lot about the modern ditto country woman. But I fair glowed with pride twice to-day. Halla said I was a (untranslateable adjective—nearest approach "fine" country-wench and Gisli the 14 year old grinned & said it was going well when I was sweating away at the hay from 7.–9. 30 non-stop. And yesterday was glorious. Up lateish—after 9. And only dinner to help get ready & washing-up & a little sweeping. And Sunday dinner—& I was in the sitting-room with the guest—her sweetheart (I think) & Páll. And at 2. 30 P.M. off we set on horse-back! It had poured all morning something terrific & all night but cleared like April with blue sky & dark clouds & a terrific wind. And I rode Haki the best horse in this district—you have to hold tight—he flies like the wind. Lord—it was good. And we called on the schoolmaster & he & his wife said I spoke *ágætliga* (excellently) & didn't believe I'd not been 2 months here which cheered me because it *is* a damn hard language. I'd forgotten the grammar was so difficult & have been disappointed I can't speak better than I seem to. Then on the folk who own the experimental seed-station—acres of oats, rye & barley blowing in the south west gale—a rose out, pansies & marigolds—Sámsstaðir. Then on Páll's niece at Þverá where again we got coffee & cakes. Then on the folk at Mulakoti to get my sandshoes—& again got coffee for the 3[d] time! (But what with riding & all it's welcome).

And home about 9. 30. PM. Supper—washed up—after guest too who came very late. Talked till 12. 15. am. bed at 12. 30. & read till almost 2. am! (So no wonder I was sleepy when I began raking at 4. P.M. after having worked almost 8 hours already! But time simply flies.) Now a wee read & then sleep, sleep, sleep. How fat I wax here—but I do be that hale & hearty. And Spain seems a long, long way off.

Wednesday 11. P.M.

Brrr–rr—cold and I'm not going to wash! I can only *either* night or morning in my room anyway so to-night I chose to-morrow morning! It's rained no end since two days ago—my wig what rain. The yard of course is a mud-mire-bog impossible to poke nose out of doors sans rubber boots & *hot* porridge is good at nights. And most of us have had slight colds (mine just in me throat) but it's been good again. The latest "new" job was helping churn butter yesterday in an old wooden pump-churn—you just bump a pole with a splay-end up & down in a narrow wooden high cone-like box and—hope for the best & the best comes sudden-like. Also—small boys of 4 are just like babies I discovered & in the midst of changing & washing one— came two folk from Lancashire to ask if I was there. When finished (being so of course involved a going to the manure-heap at the back) I entered into converse & found they were quite at sea with a prop & stay in the shape of a girl who'd had 11 "hours" of English once! So—we fixed up to "expedite" with Thorsmörk the next fine day— if one ever comes now—& I went out a short while with 'em—it was 6. PM when they arrived & I was just off to the "meadows" on the mountain with the men's coffee. One can't ride at all tho': she'll never get the whole way so we'll go slow at first & leave her half-way at a farm. The river is dangerous—with a powerful current & only for them as can stick on—I trust I can. Then—washing-up and odds & ends—darning & so forth & coffee at 11. PM with Halla whose birthday she suddenly remembered it was. To-day, Wednesday, house-jobs—washing-up (much—very much of great pots & pans in the stream—the kind with rice-porridge & gravy that's all stuck & hard)—hurrah—because it ceased to rain & even looked as tho' to-morrow might be fine. And I sallied over to the "Lancashire Lasses" (about 45 and 50 I should guess—one an inspector of elementary schools taught cooking once t'other in Manchester teaching French Spanish & German—very live—black hair brown eyes, humorous been to Russia, Romania, Lappland .... I liked 'em both because they looked as tho' they'd never do the sort of thing they are doing & there's much to both of 'em—real Lancashire folk—very like some Icelanders methinks. I went over on "Old Bruni" the biggest horse they have—alone ah–ha—& all was well 'cept that he was damn hard to get up on to ∴ Icelandic saddles don't stay put like English ones—they slide down your near side unless you're terrible quick—& the moment your foot is in the stirrup away goes your horse! But I rode with one foot in stirrup & the saddle all crooked for a bit & then managed to waggle the saddle straight—so I live & learn & didn't fall off—& had opened "gates" in bogs en route. Well—well—then I darned more & looked after Thorir (the 5-year old "not there" who wdn't go to sleep) & washed up and—talked a bit with Páll about Icelandic plays & A "Winter's Tale" & "12th Night—and so to bed. How I'd love the sun to shine again!

Friday. 11. a.m. c.

I'm in Mulakot the farm with telephone etc: and finishing this off so that you get it before I arrive meself. The Nice folk from Lancs. are posting it for me from Edinboro'. One is going to look up Maisie—she teaches languages in Central School, Manchester—a live wire—*60* & I put her down at 45 at first!!) & she rides a horse and all gaily. Maisie & she will get on fine. She'll dry up & do anything in the house. We rode all day—blazing sun—to Thorsmörk over absolute waste desert into a wood & glacier after glacier high above & beyond—lovely. Now—wet again—but yesterday *was* a day. Did few chores before leaving and bed at 1. am. after coming back. Muchest love to you—Páll & Halla *are* splendid people. How I've been gallivanting this week tho'—must make up for it now—when I get back home this morning. Jean.

On the quayside

VII

August 31. 1936.
11. 30 PM.

Good & early—Halla said I could hop it at 11. c. so hop it I did. Well, well what hasn't happened since Thursday, when I did the expedition to Thórsmörk with the two "old ladies" as the other two English (girls) who appeared here Sat' called 'em! That was heavenly—never shall I forget the sight of those glaciers—& the luxuriousness of the little birch-wood after that trek over stones—great giant pebbles—& those swirling glacier torrents—I did go slightly giddy in the middle once but looked up & along & all was well—it's a queer sensation—deafening rush of water round your boots & the horse feeling his way backing agin it and it seems he's being carried miles down—actually it's only a few yards. And, as stated, I was let go alone! Well—that was that day—only clearing away & washing-up & getting this bed & room ready for the less confident one of the two who didn't feel up to the half-hour to Mulakot in the dark—bed some time before 1. a.m. Then Friday—walked to M. with her & talked much with 'em both & stayed for lunch & so home—to wash up and bake, (took 3 hours that time 7–10 P.M.), and oh yes ironing came first for a couple of hours. Saturday, world's worst cold developed furioso—head hot & all tight—but what a day's work in spite of it all—washed socks, pots, sausage (one huge 'un wot'd been smoked & got coated 1/2 inch deep in sort fat which I had to remove in cold drops from the tap! Then also—*did* rooms (heard 2 English girls arriving—turned out of mine—bag & baggage washed floor, made beds (not as simple as in England, you try wrestling with a "sæng" (floppy eiderdown wot has to be fitted into a "shape" envelope & tied up & shook out smooth. Washed up, minded children—bloody noses & lost socks & cold-streaming noses—(while I was having 1/2 hour "off" reading part of a play—! First—Thorir had to be washed—face & hands—then Siggi warned not to wet his trousers (but he allus does!) Then Thorir fell & hurt his nose—more washing. Then Halla *did* the farm—cleared out cellar while I churned butter. But I thought she said I was to put t'other hand on the spinning kettle-like object her churn is—so I did & churned for 1/2 hour with the sweat pouring down into me mouth even—gosh it was hard—I sat & stood & propped meself up agin things—and nowt happened. Then she came & realised what was amiss—the butter came in 10 mins after that—

but I turned with such vigour I broke a bolt thing which had kept falling out before (that's very Icelandic—the handle to my door dangles from a nail in the wall of the next room on a bit of string— & the W.C. door has long since simply lain flat outside agin the wall so—"take up thy door as thou enterest"). Well—then I washed windows—in a tcupful of *originally* warm water. & dried 'em after. Then the girls arrove & had to be talked to & while they were out I got supper ready for 'em & had it with 'em. Then huge piles to wash up—lots of stuff from the fields—done about midnight—& then mended me riding-breeks wot ad "split" in two places—& so to bed, but had to sleep with mouth wide open—cdn't breathe for cold also right ear ached—but slept quite a bit. Sunday morning washed up & got their lunch (chicken-soup & chicken & I had it with 'em at 11. am!) ∵ they'd contemplated going same expeditn as we did Thursday. But it was raining so they had to cancel it. Washed up all there was (the others' things too) changed & set out with Páll & Ólafur (for Mullakot & then) to a gorgeous cleft up the dale with a waterfall dropping sheer 100 feet & more—& trees overhanging & a long gorge twisting & broadening—& the sun came out & the glacier emerged from mist & t'was good. I felt it was kill or cure the cold & if I had to work I was going to play as well. Then off to a Sunday Ball—at schoolmaster's house—in the big room in the school. Everybody from far & near there—& about 200 horses in field—good sight in the sun. Schoolmaster & wife gave us coffee & we talked, (I could scarcely, all þ's were their t's but it wasn't worse & the head was better out in the air & I was riding Haki who goes like the wind I had to hold in like mad all the way back—he got too hot on the way there. Then they danced in the thing—scene like a Bar in the Middle West in America (or is it Far West?) but not the rowdyism—at least not while we were there—girls much impressed by savoir-faire of Icelandic peasant lads who asked 'em to dance without the slightest embarassment etc: One was Joan Scott (Westmoreland & acts as hostess to Dominion students in London) t'other Janet Wood who's studying singing Chelsea—lives in Croydon I think—nice young things both of 'em, specially Joan Scott who's been brought up on horses all her life (but says English ones easier to ride—I think NOT but we'll see when I get back. How I love riding, & how Maisie would enjoy careering along on Haki. Well—the sunset on the glacier was a grey-rose flush—& a primrose moon came out above the snow flush for a few moments before it rose into clouds (I've only seen it twice since I came to Iceland but I did see green curtains of Northern Lights dancing about here twice). And we rode over to a farm where there was still an old *baðstofa* sitting-room—i.e. room with low wood-gable roof (steepish pitch) & rows of lock-wood beds (3 a side) & in which everything used to go on—no means of heating cept closed windows—& folk just sat on their beds—spinning, weaving, mending tools—knitting, bearing children, eating etc: etc. Also kitchen— black as pitch—& filled with nice sort of smoke from dried sheep dung—just a hearth & cauldrons on it—nowt else—& a delightful woman there who received us with much dignity. Olafur wants to paint it (he's the inn-keeper (but no drinks) at Mulakot & paints as a hobby—his biggest is in a big elementary school outside Reykjavík. Then home in the moonlight—11. P.M. eat egg & rye-bread & so to bed c. 12. 30 after talk about the day. Páll told us the legend about Bliksá the place where we saw the gorge—while we were there— There's nowt that man doesn't know! To-day *Monday*. Up 8. 45— Páll walked into my room he [came] to get his screw tobacco—forgot I wasnt in my own room!—then washed socks, & washed up—& then out to the mts to rake. (Had a better night tho' cold very heavy still—) & raked in blazing sun for bit—then it turned cold, put on shoes & stockings & coat. About 6. P.M. heard that Prof. Bassett had arrived. Nipped on the horse Thorir used to lead the train of hay home & bolted down the mountain home—queer riding in gym-shoes & a frock—not much to grip with but he went O.K. & I'd not been on him before—found Prof. B. & Brian his 16 yr old lad encamped— & asked about designs—They want to see Thórsmörk. Got them a meal—baked rye-cakes for 1¾ hrs—chatted a bit about their experiences—once a bus broke down & they arrived miles away from Reykjavik where most folk wanted to go at 4 *am* instead of 9. P.M.! Also—nearly into a river because the earth on road gave way at a crucial bend. Slept on café floor that night. Then—put Siggi to bed (had to be 1st coaxed & washed—coaxing a bit difficult in Icelandic but it went OK.) & he broke a porridge-plate before. Washed up large piles again—& 11. PM. or just after—to bed, to bed. Cold a bit better— rubbed feet with castor-oil (remedy I've just heard of from the "old ladies)—Bassett much tickled at my present way of life—it must strike an outsider & one unfamiliar with ways Icelandic as a trifle odd—I quite see—but I've imbibed much—Anna indeed spoke of "foreigners" to me & I laughed, ∴ I'm one too but not quite she says ∴ of speaking & working with them. It's fun to "belong"—now I must sleep.

Wednesday.

Well, I dunno what Prof. Bassett thinks of my mode of life now—last time I saw him I handed him—"the guests' chamber-pot"! I think he & his 16 year old son were more embarassed than I was—I was NOT—& told 'em its name in Icelandic to make 'em feel more Icelandic about it. The reason being it's coming down in torrents & all their spare clothes they usually sleep in & on & about are wet through ·.· they went to Thórsmörk—& got caught in this depression. They arrived about 9. P.M. & after pulling off their boots (he wore mine & I thought he'd *never* get out—he sitting on Gisli's bed & I sticking one leg round the door to get purchase to tug with—hanging up their trousers chiefly over the electric fire in my room—giving 'em said room to change in—feeding 'em on hot porridge bread & eggs & coffee—they decided it was too rough a night for the 16 yr old to face—so we hauled the divan from my room into another next door (Gisli's is the entrance-hall to both—so is an Icelandic house arranged—& then they both sleep with the cupboard containing the extra clothes of Páll & Halla—the iron and rickety ironing table, some spare bedding & a desk. Since—I've washed up & made merry with Halla over the way one gets better acquainted with one's compatriots when abroad. And before that I'd been working all day since 8. 30. washing-up, baking rye-cakes (lovely—I sat on a bench doing it for almost 1½ hrs—nice rest), darning socks with holes you could put your whole *foot* through, looking after Siggi (who didn't wet his trousers for the very first day since he's come—I kept asking him if he wanted to "pissa"—& Thorir who was in a mischievous mood, while darning socks & put him to bed just before they came. Poured with rain so no raking for me, & swept floors & chased cows from hay bagga & made bannocks for 'em. Cold a bittie better. Yesterday—got the Bassett pair's meals (I do the setting of table etc:) & washed up—dressed Siggi—& washed up & baked and then at 3. 30 out to the hay-meadows miles up the mountain—in a drizzle & a howling N.E. gale which fairly tossed the hay about. Home—(wore a bit of sheep's fleece I found lying about as a cap t'was for once too chill to be entirely bareheaded as I've been allus since I set foot on Icelandic soil) feeling the cold a trifle—I wish it'd hurry up & go I'm bored with it & it's very difficult (indoors) when you've only *4* hkfs altogether—outside you do as the Icelanders do—but revived after hot porridge. Gave the B's their meal, talked, gave the men from the fields theirs'—washed up everything, to bed about 11. 15—early for once. Now—nearly 1. am. must sleep. I think I'll be wise & have a whole day in bed when I get to Reykjavík. Páll & Halla are being splendid to the B's—Páll himself took 'em to Thórsmörk a thing he's not done all summer. They are nice people.

Saturday. 11. 30. pm.

Well—nice to sit down. Didn't at all to-day 'cept for meals from time I got up!!! Dressed infants, washed up (all the stuff from "the meadows"—i.e. tin pail, wooden pail, enamel cans spoons forks & knives wot had to be cleaned as in the good old days with an inch of emery paper. Then washed window & door ledges chairs (all woodwork in the sitting-room (which accounts for the faded look of much Icelandic paint!), got the B's meals (they've fair enjoyed their week here I think), fed infants (literally) washed-up (Halla baking most of the time) got B's more meals, gave men porridge & milk when they came in from the fields, washed oven-plates, washed-up, swept floors, made beds, washed up, (*NB it allus includes all the drying as well*) washed cloths, scoured pots (poured all day so no stream—all done under 1 tap which drips at rate of a teaspoonful per second only!) But it has its advantages when you're washing lettuce or spinach. I've discovered. Washed up and scoured sink with boiling soda-water. And so & so & so to bed. And yesterday—was much like cept that at 2. P.M. I did set off for "the meadows"—& made hay gently—down in the bog squelch-squelch in a glorious weather (the sun was *hot* in the morning) and felt strong & hearty, the cold being that much better—no tight head or ear or throat, hooray. Made hay till about 7. 30. p.m. & the light on the glacier with a new covering of snow I'll not forget soon—nor the blue hills up the dale. Then home, gave B's their supper & baked rye-cakes all the time & gave men porridge (& ate mine while baking) & washed up & washed up & washed up. But Thursday was different—I had the day off—that is in the afternoon off we set for the place where they grow oats & wheat & barley & rye Sámsstaðir & the air was fresh & cold & it cleared up after rain— & there was new snow on the glaciers & on the jagged dark blue peaks that suddenly stuck up round a bend in the road—over brilliant green grass—lord it was beautiful. And the rye waved tall as a man agin all that & the great glacier—& didn't I understand why Gunnar of Lithend (in Njálssaga couldn't bear to leave his home when he'd been outlawed & stayed—& got killed by his enemies. Then we visited the farm with the old baðstofa (I thought the B's d like to see it—& the folk were charming & offered us coffee which we refused having already partaken of it at S.) And then—to the schoolhouse where the schoolmaster's wife gave us coffee (we were chilly & it was good as it was 8. 30. p.m.) It's glorious riding all afternoon like that—easily & drinking in the loveliness & *watching* other folk work in the hay-fields. And behold coming home—a full moon behind mackerel clouds & it gradually swung clear so that the snow on the glacier gleamed blue—& we rode & rode—feet froze, the night was so keen—& home—at a gallop the last patch of grass—by the hundred & one great and little waterfalls roaring & splashing down—the best ride I've yet had almost. But the one you've just had is always the best. But still to ride in moonlight with a blue glacier aglow ahead & white falls crashing on your left & a great expanse of stone & sand lit up by river-tracks shining in the light is an experience. Fed hugely on sour meat, rye-bread, eggs, smoked sausage, bits of veal (new meat) & coffee—washed up & bed about 2. am. much content. It's days like these that are so lovely & Páll & Halla just let me off like that horse & all which is most decent of 'em. That's two whole weekdays I've had "free" thus since I came. And ideas about this farm change—the B's said they didn't think much of it at 1st but I guess they do otherwise now—they had the best parlour to themselves all day & it pouring cats & dogs & it'd have been no fun at all in a tent.) Halla fights the mess with all her might but there's just too much for her to do. In how many English farms is all the woodwork *washed* of a Saturday afternoon I wonder—& windows & chandeliers & all? And the men have a good wash in a minute enamel basin—heads & all. And—well, well, well, don't they have an electric stove too—but when you think that there's only one woman to run it all—cook, *wash*, clean, churn, milk, bake—(even the meat is kept away up the hill in a cellar place). I know now what it must have been like for the Ancient Icelandic Female from my own experience—no wonder she was often as she was. Now—I'm leaving on Tuesday I think. I'd thought I might stay the week out but now to-day came a letter from Clo (Miss Clover of Cambridge) to ask me cd I possibly go to Stykkisholm (up in the N.W.) to visit a schoolhouse where Dame Bertha's books are (she gave 'em all those the Univ. Lib^y & G.C. didn't get). And I feel I must & wd like to do that—it'll be a pleasant expedition—& I'd like another now after this "rest-by-the-way"! So off I hop—& then for a "quiet time" in Reykjavik (?) before sleeping all the way home.

Sunday. 12. 15. *a.m.*

Bed again—after a glorious day! Wild wet windy night but no rain early m^g. Then up c. 9. am. and got the B's coffee & helped get their lunch ready & then ate mine with t'others in kitchen—salt meat & thick gravy potatoes followed by pink fruit porridge but for me skyr (sour milk) hourly—it's so much nicer. Then washed up, changed & ready by 2. p.m. for the excursion across the river-desert to a particularly beautiful waterfall—about 3 hrs riding fairly hard. Poured with drizzle-rain at first & looked black but after we reached the fall it cleared. Anyway it was lovely seeing the greens—what a variety there are of green colours here—through the mist & being on horseback. I rode Haki again—lord how good it is to ride, ride, ride. And the fall was joyous—it sprang clear & fell sheer in a spouting stream—and you could get in behind it—120 feet back or so in a sort of vault & see almost the whole 250 feet of it fall sheer & spray rising like the steam from a geysir & it tossing about on the surface—what a fall. Then out onto the grass again & away at full canter in quest of coffee which we had about 6. 30. p.m. at a farm where the mud is bout as thick & deep as it is here. Then gallop over bog & mud tracks & through streams to the largest rowan tree in Scandinavia (I shd say Europe too). It grows out of a crack in a rock & its trunk is enormous & it overhangs a deep gorge with a stream rushing below. You can walk across on its branches that span the gulf. And then down to the *fljot* once more into the Thorsmörk onto *black*-blue through shifting mist & the grass brilliant yellow-green. And we raced through the glacial streams—I wasn't a bit scared this time—wished they'd been deeper & the current more! One was fairly strong—& there were quicksands the guide's horse sank into once—but he got out—black quaking wastes—rather nasty & sts there are in the rivers which makes the fording a trifle difficult. There were about twenty or more glacier streams to get over so t'was quite fun. And the going over the shingle much easier than to Thorsmörk where you're picking your way over boulders so often. Gallop a gallop home with rain coming on again—& a good supper of hot porridge, spinach & egg & salted mutton & bread & coffee & milk (I fed with them). Washed up—& then Halla asked me about going away—she's an awful lot to do this coming week—the B's have of course hung up things like washing—& there's much to do out in the fields too—& they've been terribly decent about letting me ride—I've done more in my 3 weeks here than all the rest of my stay in Iceland & they're glorious horses—

Haki the best for miles & miles—so I'm staying after all till next week. I don't really need so long in Reykjavík—I can always read at home & I feel that there's been so much to do with English folks these last 10 days that Icelandic has stood still—if not gone back & I've seen less of the folk here—and don't want to leave thus—so all is well. I'll do the Stykkisholm j^y as quickly as possible & there'll still be 4 whole days in Reykjavik. And I shd like a last Sunday here alone with the Icelanders. Good-night.

Monday. 11. P.M.

Early for once. To-days report—*WASHED UP!* Just dealt with the pails & cans from the meadows & all clean—even linoleum wot serves as draining-boards wiped. It rained, it is raining, & it will continue to rain—oh I darned socks for 10 mins some time this evening & sat chatting 20 mins with the B's. I wish I had a tougher hide—I do be all cuts etc: & a queer whitlow like finger but I squeezed it & it's better this evening. Dunno quite why I said I'd stay now, but there's a queer fascination about all this—& anyway I've burned me boats now—& a month is a real test. Good-night.

Tuesday. *10. 40. P.M.*!

NOT 11. even & I'm *in bed*—washed up & all & "explained" his bill to Prof. Bassett who's off to-morrow after a 9 day stay here. These last two days have been a bit dreary for 'em I'm afraid—just rain & rain & more rain & it's not so noticeable if you're busy—I've not been out cept to scour the porridge-pot in the stream (clad in oil-skins!) And to-day I spent much time with 'em gossiping after meals—two of which I ate with them. I like B.—his son (16) Brian spent most of the time sleeping on the sofa in sitting-room or in the hay-loft. We talked Iceland, holidays, books & a spot about Reading which again begins to loom up instead of being far, far away. Cold much better & pleasant to be about & finger improved tho' hot a bit to-night—I'll put a new dressing on it. Wouldn't it be nice if Siggi, for once, didn't wet his trousers etc:! And I ask him every time I see him. Well, well. And Bói licked the Brisling tin to-night—without damaging his tongue. They've no sweets of course out here so sardine-tins & new potatoes & raw turnips take their place. I must send a box from Reykjavík for the boys. Well—this'll likely be the last letter you'll get from this country—& it brings you muchest love. I hope all was well if that Swedish girl turned up from Reading. And

Eleanor isn't going to take the job—so you can let her know I did get her letter day before yesterday only—no Sat^y—I *may* bring home an Icelander—to cook & clean for you in return for her food but it's not at all certain. Only for a bit & we'll find somewhere else she can go later—she's a capable lass in the kitchen & young & spritely. Aged 20. (I'll stand her keep). Phew—how it rains—poor Bassetts packing a wet tent to-morrow. I'll walk to Mulakot where the bus goes from if it's fine—nice to get out but better to be indoors the like of this weather. Then—an enormous washing to get done this week sometime—followed by ditto ironing but I hope I get out into the fields once more—if good weather comes. How very odd it'll be to cease being "Johanna" & turn into a Miss Young from England instead of Paul's "Danish help from England" as I've been termed here once (they tend to call all foreigners Danes! like the Empire Butter joke). While baking rye cakes to-day or wasn't it yesterday I had an idea about my Inter lekks which was encouraging—I want to change 'em & improve 'em. Well—well—good-night—keep well & I hope the weather's better chez-vous—but it's not been at all bad here altogether—& the really good days are simply glorious because of glaciers & green grass & waterfalls & space.

                                                                    Jean.
What fun this all is & what fun to come back to a different life again too—this has been like taking part in an exciting film, but *real*.

Trekking

VIII

11. 30. PM. Wednesday 9/9/36.

Just had a bright idea about late hours here—"an hour before midnight worth two after" etc:—well the clock here is 1½ hr in advance of the real time "wireless time" as they call it (so we can be out late for the hay—it isn't dark till after 9.)—so that 11. 30 is really only 10 P.M. (tho' of course by "wireless time" we were up at 6. a.m!) so that we do get in two hours before midnight. Just now the rain is lashing down agin the corrugated iron roof and it's well we got the hay in that was only mowed this m^g. I began at 7. 30 (or 6. a.m.) and escorted the B's to catch their bus from the the farm 2½ mls away. Lovely m^g—wild but sun trying to break through and the blue glacier mts glorious agin brilliant green grass. Chatted with nice old Guðbjörg the inn-keeper's mother (the inn-keeper paints as a hobby—quite well), then called in on another old lady Astrid & Professor Gordon of Manchester know—then home & washed up. Then helped get dinner ready—ah–me—took me pots to the stream & dealt with 'em there with great joy & satisfaction. Then washed socks—about 18 in all this time soaked with mud—and they needed much banging on the flat stone with the wood clapper. Then went to fetch Thorir (the 5 yr old) from the flat bit where they were working to-day about a mile away west (they allus talk about E. & W. even in the house here—isn't it pleasant?) & they all came back—& the walk through the air was good (it rained so Mon. & Tues. I wasn't out at all). Then dinner—usual salt fish & potato & turnip & rice pudding. WASHED UP & then out to make hay about 5. P.M. Terrific wind sprang up—kind that made your nose drip even tho' you hadn't a cold so mine did quite a lot (but it's almost gone at last that cold). Wind got stronger so it was almost impossible to rake—& we fought our way home agin it—Coffee out—rather cold ∴ Halla brought it with Thorir & it took a long time to come. On way home colouring glum—kind you get before a storm—livid greens & blues & black clouds over the dale & glacier—& queer shifting yellow light across the stone-waste where the rivers run. And the waterfalls running like milk. And a bit of a rainbow leaping right out of the glacier. Baked cakes for about two hours—while Halla & Anna began to wash (in a big zinc bath just at me elbow) & milked the cows. Gave me their hot porridge—had mine—and WASHED UP and H. & A. continued washing in the big bath—& so to bed at 11. PM. (Washed meself since—now very weary but much content. How queer it'll be to cease this purely physical life—it is so good & peaceful & restful—just obeying orders & working hard & eating lots & sleeping well. I wax fat.

Thursday. 11. 15. PM.

Well—we washed—I got up lateish—sleepy after the long day yesterday—& Halla began washing almost at once—wet day so her big bath & smaller with lid on the stove as it were "occupied" the kitchen. I WASHED UP and swept rooms—lor' what a dust & all feathers & hay do make—then time to send off the men's dinner in the pail & to have our own—salt meat for a change & very good I found it. Oh—first thing before washing up, I took Thórir for a walk to visit his great-aunt at the next farm & she gave him 2 lumps of sugar & off we toddled again through the fresh m^g & the sunshine (it rained afterwards). Then I helped H. rinse everything in the stream—EVERYTHING including the men's great dungarees—(what a weight!) and SACKS—just plain sacks wot'd had oats & stuff in 'em. That took till about 8. P.M.

Friday. 11. 25. PM c.

At that point the girl of 16 I'm now sharing me room with finished her ablutions so I set off on mine which were slightly more complex and lengthy! Well—"about 8. PM". Then in to feed the infants of 5 & 4 & put the 5 year old to bed & he almost fell asleep on the pot (I wondered why he was such an awful long time—I learn daily). Then gave men their supper had mine in between I think and WASHED UP. And then retired with Anna's daughter Sigrny (the 16 yr old). She's worked 2 yrs at a big confectioners in Reykjavik—bakes all their fancy stuff—& is that capable—I'd take her to be 20 at least—a nice lassie—big & bonnie—fatter even than I am at this moment—fond of dancing & acting works 6. a.m.–5–6 PM. *or* 8. a.m. –9. PM (!) for 50/- a month & gets 14 days "off" a year. My wig how they work up here—& her ankles swell up times with the many hours standing. But she's interested in her work & keen to learn more by coming abroad some time later. She's read Laxnes' book the one I've talked about a bit "Independent Folk" & thinks it good (it's a "classic" I spose we'd call it & that a 16 year old help in a baker's shop should have read it is typical of this country. I told her she'd have to dance with Hreiðar the 18 yr old to-morrow evening on Sunday he dances so well—& the wireless is allus switched on then—indeed every evening & it's pleasant to listen to whilst WASHING UP. Well—this m͞g up earlier soon after 8. and out to see the glacier emerging from mist in shifting sunlight—the green below looked so near in that light. Halla & Anna were milking their cows—Halla in blue Anna with a bright red jersey and a black overall—good colouring. Few mins thus—then breakfast & then darning of socks—out well wrapped up on the top of one of the stables—turf-grown (you see the cows wandering about the roofs at night of course). That was peaceful & good—I only heard the waterfall up stream—can see it from here—and saw the misty mountains. Then in & WASHED UP and despatched Gisli with the meadow folk's coffee. Then darned—then helped Halla hang out some of the clothes—exciting as it involved standing on tip-toe on an object like this ⬚—dunno what they use 'em for—but it bore me & the bars didn't break nor did the line. More darning—it tried to rain—dinner —fish & rice then WASHED UP—more darning. Oh—swept up two rooms & made beds some time this morning—took in clothes from a terrific shower (it continued to rain heavily after that)—chased cows from garden, darned, then ironed till about 8. PM. Then gave small infant supper (feeding one) put him to bed, had my supper— & sat down a wee while—then WASHED UP and—so—to—bed. I just don't know what happens to the time here—Friday & my "extra" week here almost over. Do hope to-morrow or Sunday's fine too for the last sight of the place. It wallows in *green* mud at the moment (from stables etc:) & the best way of getting to & from the stream is by walking along the turf & stone wall of the garden & giving the yard a miss but that takes time so can't allus be done. Made up me mind too to try to see Laxnes & tell him I'd like to translate his book for him, (if it's still "free" for English folk—it's been done into German already), feel I'd be able to after this month ∴ now I know about this kind of life 1st hand & from inside. We'll see. Can't believe that at the end of this month only a fortnight now I'll be back in England & picking up the dropped threads of a very different existence. It's been such fun to be "Johanna at Árkvörni." It'll sound queer to be called Jean or Miss Young again. And how very odd not to be called for & sent to do this, that & t'other. Páll very sympathetic about desire to translate Laxness—see little of him of course because I've been indoors all this week—bad weather & better so— very wet raking. But there's lots of hay cut so I may be out tomorrow. Good-night. Sigrny is reading.

Sunday ? a.m.
Too weary to scribble yesterday which ended about midnight. It began by Halla bending over me & saying sg about a very beautiful rainbow—I leaped up put overall over pyjamas and out—and it was glorious. Spanned the whole stretch of country to the west—began up the hill quite near & arched right out to sea and a complete *double* one—with very high apex—& the sun gleaming on the glacier to the south & east—well I got up after contemplating that—& climbed the hill to the pool under the little fall—cold but that invigorating & refreshing to have a bath—soaped all over first—did feel clean. Then—hung out rest of washing to dry—took time as it involved fetching from grass by stream where it'd been lying (on dishcloths) & stretching up on rickety box affair for bedspreads & sheets. But good to be out in *sun* once more—mist about and a little rain but not much till evening, washed muddy socks—stripped some beds—then breakfast—took a few snaps of this place & of Halla & Thorir (the little 5 yr old who looks quite normal when he's laughing). Then WASHED UP and baked rye-cakes and then, really because I'd strongly hinted I'd like to rake this last day in the good sun and all— set off in boots & oilskin coat tied round middle plus gym-shoes plus woolly plus camera—for the meadows—now almost an hour's walk away! And—the sun was pure joy—and I lay me down & rested a few minutes en route & took snaps of one of the myriad falls spouting from the cliff-way—also of the glacier that was good with clouds & a little mist trailing away east. So I arrived on the field of action a trifle late but feeling fresh—& raked with interval for dinner & coffee until after 8. p.m. And it was good. Grand to be out in that good air. I slept a bit after dinner in the wind & sun (cold tho' the wind was) and that was good to do. And the walk home through coming twilight with black rain ahead & the grey river ripping through the black sand just the sound of the waterfalls & the curlews gathering to move south was very good indeed. Got home & first gave Thorir his porridge & egg (which he wdn't eat) & put him to bed and changed bed-clothes—then ate my porridge & excellent chunks of rye-bread & dripping plus a bit of smoked sheep-sausage—then sorted out meadow-stuff (spoons forks tin pail etc:) and WASHED UP—including pail etc: which I took down to stream in black night with me overall to rinse. Did knives with emery paper, cleaned sink with boiling soda water—washed me overall & socks & stockings & then it was 11. P.M. Paul came into kitchen & talked

about plays chiefly & I told him about Macbeth and Pirandello's "As You desire me" which he didn't know. And so—to—bed—& it's lashing with rain. And it's pelting now but I don't think it'll be impossible to get out—hope not at anyrate. Think I'll get up—so wide awake now.
Well that's it—

          Reykjavík. Tuesday 10. a.m.(!)
Well—well—well. To-day feels like a huge blank sheet of paper and I can write just what I will on it losh! But what a month I've had—it's as if I'd been re-incarnated pro tem. And it's odd and good to think I can lepp into that existence again one day if I will—tho' of course now I know 'em at Árkvörn it won't ever be quite the same again. Well—Sunday was good. I woke as you know earlyish and went to borrow the mincer from the farm half a mile away to the east. And old Sigriðr (who nursed Prof. Gordon of Manchester when he was staying with her once & got asthma) had a pair of gloves (designated for Eleanor or praps I'll keep 'em ∵ Sigriðr knitted 'em & hoped *I'd* wear 'em tho' I told her I wanted 'em for a friend) and I'll get Eleanor a pair here—) ready for me and wdn't take more than 4/- tho' here they're allus at least 5/- —and I ordered another pair (praps for Irène) I don't think you cd do with 'em ∵ they've no fingers but they're that warm & soft & a good pattern & the colour of the sheep here. Then I minced with Anna down in the cellar—it took over an hour—had to be put through three times (the result when you eat it is delicious) ∵ the salt stuff is so grisly and fat & when it's soft it oozes out *that* slow. We got almost cross & then I felt ashamed ∵ that's such a minor thing really—and when I contemplate what Halla puts up with in the way of a tap that drips only etc: etc:—Well—then H. said I'd better say good-bye to old Sigriðr (who's Páll's aunt) then as we might be late that evening so off I went again after cleaning the mincer in the stream & then with a cupful of boiling water (from the potato-pot). And we chatted over coffee & cakes (at 12. p.m.) Laura S's daughter & I & of course like everybody else L. wts to come to England. I hope by the way that that girl Finna doesn't & that Sofía does—she may instead. She's Guðbjörg of Mulakot's daughter & a fine person is Guðbjörg. Then Gísli came to say that Páll was ready & they'd had dinner so I ran back & bolted the minced-meat & spinach & skýr (H. knew I liked that better than rhubarb-cornflower-porridge) & changed & out we

rode to Kollabær beyond the schoolhouse & had coffee about 5. 30. p.m. Then home—and more & more folk joined us especially at Mulakot. And there was mist driving about the glacier but the grass glowed green and the pale sun struck the river so that it changed from pewter to silver—all its myriad streams & channels amongst the grey black sand & stone waste. Lord, lord, how I loved it all—and the waterfalls crashing down the hillside all the way back, and the horses tossing their manes as we passed—the untamed ones—they never tame 'em till they're 4 yrs old here—that's why they're so good I think & the taming is very gradual & slow. And from Mulakot home the last two miles I let Haki rip—and tho' there were 11 of us there & some of the men had "lively" horses—Haki just outstripped 'em all—and we charged over the hummocks. I've never had such a "val-hopp" gallop before and enjoyed it to the full. I think Haki knew it was the last ride and he felt the thrill coming through the saddle and me boots! And the farmer who came second asked with a grin if I'd often ridden like that—and wasn't Haki a joy to ride. The snag is that next time I'm on at home I'll forget I'm not on an Icelandic beastie and I'll find meself on me head on the ground. Well, then half the farmers came in for coffee and Halla & Anna & I served—and we ate porridge & rye-bread & mince-meat spread—and put Thórir to bed—with the door open to join in the talk. There was some of dancing but they were oldish fellows most of 'em so rather to the chagrin of Anna's 16 yr old daughter who changed nowt came of it. Then washed up for last time and then packed. And Halla gave me a bit of stuff she'd spun & Páll had woven—like their chair-covers in the "parlour" & it'd make a cushion-cover & I'll use it at Reading at the U^y. It's lovely to have just *that*. And Páll gave me the new illustrated edition of Laxdæla Saga—a rare book & bound and all—with "To Johanna, with thanks for the summer from Páll" in it. They didn't oughter do sich things. And Anna ironed my overall that I washed partly in stream & partly at home, before bed. And so and so and so after talk to bed. I slept not very much—in view of going and all—but felt spry in the m^g & went out to say good-bye to the men—Páll & Thori and Hreiðar & they all said "thank you for good company" (as they do here) and I watched 'em plod up the hill & up the mountain with the ropes & the enamel can of porridge & Páll waved at the turn. And then Anna milked—and the yellow sunlight began to flood the green tún and the great waste beyond—and the mist to shift over the glacier & Halla called me in to breakfast—of many kinds of bread & an egg & smoked sausage & cakes & coffee. Then—she decided to ride with me to Mulakot—my baggage was rather heavy as it contained about 2¾ lbs of wool for a friend of Eleanor's plus book from Páll now—& she rode the colt Hreiðar has been taming a beautiful animal but still wild but all went well & so that was one more ride—I rode in me tartan skirt which is so gloriously wide & only scratched a leg agin some barbed wire fencing going through a gate for me laziness—the opening was narrow & I'd a rooky 30 lbs & a bag on me shoulders & behind me & bumped a bit as we rode. And the sun came still farther out—and at Mulakot old Guðbjörg gave me a bouquet of flowers from her garden— Marigolds, then deep deep crimson Sweet Williams, then some other old-fashioned white flowers—then blue pansies—a Victorian bunch— in concentric circles as it were—also some "everlasting" flowers (pinkish with yellow centres and rather like big paper daisies) to take home to England. And "Vertu nú blessuð og sæl" (Be you now blessed and happy" (a good salutation which they give when they know you well or you're a relative) & off went the bus. But it stuck in the mud round the corner of the farm and Siggi the driver had to get a spade & dig it out. At the next farm got in old Erlendr Erlendsson the old man of 81 who was hopping about at the "Ball" in the schoolhouse yon Sunday. He was coming to Reykjavik (1st time he'd left his farm I believe) for his sister's funeral—she was 79) and we sat together & chatted all the way & I gave him half my chocolate I bought at Ölfusaá stop—when I went to wash my boots in the torrent—Thorsá ?Olfusá—my wig what a river—swirling & racing & milky-green-grey, and Ingolfsfell standing up dark blue & misty under a grey sky. It'd been raining there. But the first few hours were best—never have I seen so clearly—and Hekla which is hardly ever clear—stood out quite naked from the plain in brilliant sunshine & then Búrfell & the Þríhyrning (Three Corner Mtn) & the range leading up to Eyjafjalla glacier which was half hidden in clouds. Lord—lord—& the distance t'other side all waste & here & there a queer pink colour. Then the wind got up & it grew chillier & it had rained much as we came west—splashing through the pools—& up on Svínahraun (Swine Lava Field) mist and green shining grass amongst the lava—& Reykjavik grey & the wind swirling paper about. And the rutebil took me right to the door of the nice chimney-sweep's. And it was almost like coming home they welcomed a body so and I told 'em a bit—and had coffee & then went out to shop—

lots of presents to give all the folk who've been so nice to me—(I'd like to send from home but a) there's customs problems—everything is duty-able and b) I'll not have time once I plunge into this year at Reading—)—& then discovered I'd forgotten money (∴ I've not used any for over a month now!) so wandered about a few mins deciding what I'd buy. And then a voice said "Hullo are you here" (in Icelandic) and there was big Bjarni from Reyðarfirth in the east— whom we met at Ásbyrgi & who took such good snaps. He said he thought I was in England by now & I said far from it & told him what I'd done since Ásbyrgi (in July was it?) & we drank coffee & talked an hour & then it was time for the evening meal with the nice chimney-sweep (they've just said I can go there any time I like for meals & it's so much more fun being with folk & they talk less fast & more distinctly than the country-folk—tho' there are no "dialects" here) And I dried up. It felt so odd to sit down at a tablecloth & to have so many utensils—plates & saucers & what not—& then the water just gushed from their tap. And altogether it was most pleasant—for a change. Then at 9. pm I decided bed was the one & only place & I cdn't face the thought of going to Stykkisholm or any other holm for a day or two—so here I be—after nearly an hour's scribbling to you. I may go Friday but if I can find out what's happened exactly about Dame Bertha's books here I'd rather spend this last week peacefully in Reykjavík. My wig I was weary last night & slept till 8. a.m. & then began thinking about presents & house-hunting in Reading (!) so got up & made coffee from Mrs Særet's present Café Veige—delicious with the coffee-cream I bought from the milk shop up the street. When I got here yesterday before sallying out to shop— this is the "flat of Benedikt Jacobsson" the nice gym-instructor Ástrid knows—I found doors open—even of the clothes cupboard— someone had been in to "clean" & I slept with 'em open ∴ I'd only the key to B's room I found! It's so like Reykjavik this—anyone cd come in & walk off with anything! But no-one does. Now I must "tidy" up a spot—all my gear is strewed about—& then shop & then it'll be lunch (dinner-) time. It was odd not to hear Páll waken Gísli first-thing this morning. And what a gale last night—a terrific S.W-ester fair tearing through the town. But grey & quiet this morning. Summer is over though it's not cold at the moment. I'm posting this—you'll get it just before I come I expect. I hope by the way that I shall get home Sunday eve—27th but Prof. Bassett left a note to say

Letters from Iceland 1936

that *his* boat was a day late leaving Reykjavík so I don't know. Mine is *Goðafoss* & due to leave *23ᵈ* & sails to *Hull*. Fare thee well a wee.

c. 6. 45 PM.

Well—I must say there is sg that satisfying about spending when you haven't for over a month! I came in the other minute with exactly 2 English farthings and 1 Icelandic eyri! But I've done all me necessary shopping for presents here and got just what I wanted so feel most pleased. Also wrote Astrid pages and had coffee with Júlia another friend of hers and called on someone else who wasn't feeling very well (didn't know the complaint—it sounded like "kirtles") and so home to finish this before posting it. Haven't heard from Finna who was going to have sent a letter yesterday so may still turn up minus an Icelander—but hope that Fía will come if Finna doesn't. Also hear that *Dettifoss* was 2 days late so trust & pray my boat'll be up to time but Prof. Bassett will have warned 'em at Reading—he was on *Dettifoss*—I may have to go straight to Reading—in which case I'll come home for Wednesday night & part of Thursday—all I can do—but I don't want to miss Kathleen Steeds who'll be there the week-end before. So—praps see you Sunday–Monday 27–28—praps Wednesday 30. I'll wire on arrival in England. Muchest love to all—Jean Johanna.

Crossing the river

Geysir

Bergþórshvoll